NARCISSISM: BEHIND THE MASK

NARCISSISM: BEHIND THE MASK

David Thomas PhD

Book Guild Publishing

Sussex, England

First published in Great Britain in 2010 by
The Book Guild Ltd
Pavilion View
19 New Road
Brighton, BN1 1UF

Typesetting in Garamond by
YHT Ltd, London

Printed in Great Britain by
CPI Antony Rowe

A catalogue record for this book is available from
The British Library.

ISBN 978 1 84624 506 0

Contents

To Bill Murphy
of the University of Derby — thank you

Preface

For hundreds of years scientists peered into space at stars like our sun, wondering if they had planets orbiting them. Their telescopes could see the stars easily enough, but they weren't able to detect the planets, if they existed. It was relatively recently that the scientists found the answer.

If the star has a planet circling it, then the planet's gravity will 'wobble' the star as it circles it. The amount of wobble will be related to the mass of the planet, which pulls the star towards it through gravity as it circles. The behaviour of the star is symptomatic of its relationship with its planet.

The narcissist is like a star, in that his behaviour betrays what is going on around him – if, like the scientists, you know what to look for.

There are telltale signs in a person's behaviour at all stages of life. A mother may over-control her child, not allowing it to develop properly; the child then clings to the mother and may develop the need for her approval before performing even the simplest of tasks. Following this, for the rest of their lives, such children view the world through the eyes of their mother, living their lives according to the template she laid down.

Then there is the adolescent who shows symptoms of abuse by, for example, defending his father's offending behaviour, often to the extent of putting him on a pedestal. If he says that he was beaten by his father when he was young, he'll explain that the beatings did him no harm, that they made him the person he is today.

Abuse by parents, often unintentional and sometimes brought about by over-indulgence in the pursuit of pleasure for themselves and for their children, invariably has the unfortunate outcome of producing a child who grows into a maladjusted adult. It's not surprising that parents who don't define the boundaries for their children produce offspring who don't know where the boundaries lie. An adolescent who enters the adult world without having had guidance as to where interpersonal boundaries lie runs the risk of becoming narcissistic. An individual who develops symptoms of its worst form, malignant narcissism, can create mayhem for many innocent individuals who have the misfortune to be associated with this person during their adult life.

Unbridled narcissism is more often than not at the root of emotional pain and suffering, both for the narcissist himself and for those around him. Much of the exponential growth of narcissistic behaviour in recent times has been brought about by the influence of an uncontrolled media creating a materialistic consumer frenzy, and has fuelled a population with unrealistic aspirations that will inevitably be mostly unfulfilled. This leaves a gap in the individual between the real self and the ideal self, or between the 'I am' and the 'I should', and results in pain and suffering of the mind, often with associated periods of depression.

If we can understand narcissists and their codependent supporters, we can find ways to remove much of the pain and suffering, not only in the lives of those who suffer at their hands, but also in the lives of the narcissists themselves and in those of their codependents, and we can also reduce the frequency and depth of any ensuing periods of anxiety and depression.

This book looks at the narcissist and the codependent analytically and through study of individuals, as a way of enriching our understanding of both them and ourselves. It looks at their behaviour and relationships, their symptoms, the root causes, the meaning behind their words, why they behave as they do, why they suffer emotionally, why and how they cause pain and suffering in others, how to deal with them, and how the narcissist and the codependent and those afflicted by their behaviour can move towards gaining control and gaining or regaining happiness ... and you won't need a telescope!

Introduction

There are times in our lives, principally when we are young, when we feel particularly bad about something that is extremely emotional and painful to bear. Later, it disappears from our conscious thoughts; it seems that we have forgotten it. In fact, it has just moved from our conscious to our unconscious. For the remainder of our life, every time we are reminded of that something that was so emotional and painful to bear, it acts as a trigger to which we often can't help but react. Whether we react or not, and how aggressively we react, depends on our emotional state at the time.

It is normal for us to compare ourselves against others in all sorts of ways. For example, we may contrast our looks, our size, our intelligence, our qualifications, our possessions, and so on. If we feel superior it may give us a boost. If we feel inferior, it can make us feel a little worse.

When you are born you are inferior to your parents in terms of physical size and knowledge of the world. It takes many years to bridge the size and knowledge gap. If you are unlucky enough to have a parent who uses their superiority to boost their own confidence or self-esteem at your expense through intentional or unintentional emotional abuse – for instance, by mocking you or by imposing their will on you and not respecting your feelings – then you will develop strong feelings of inferiority which return again and again later in life and act as triggers to inform your behaviour. Without us realising it, our past is constantly determining our present actions.

The abuse can take many forms. It is widely acknowledged that severe abuse such as beatings or sexual abuse of a child will later result in a disturbed adult, often with severe emotional problems. But there are other, more subtle forms of abuse that also result in emotional problems in later life, and subtle forms of abuse of children can also frequently result in severe problems when the child becomes an adult. It is extremely difficult to make the connections between these more subtle forms of abuse and the problems experienced later in life, but it is the case that the roots of an adult life are put down during childhood.

From birth through to death, all humans seek to create a pattern for everything they look at, even if it is a completely random one. We are hardwired to find meaning and purpose throughout our lives. When we are unable to find one or the other of these it causes confusion in our mind, so we continually seek a way to understand what is going on. If we want to exercise some control over what is happening, we have to understand the reason behind these events.

A child looks for patterns and therefore meaning from very early on in life. Initially, he or she views the world as a random set of events, some or all of which are emotional. It is the child's carer, usually the mother, who imposes a pattern to these apparently random events. Healthy narcissism starts from a warm and responsive mother who accurately mirrors the child's feelings and reflects them back. The mother is responsive and attuned to the child's emotional needs. The child then develops a secure attachment to his mother and learns to know and accept himself for what he is. Over time, the child develops meaning and purpose.

If the mirroring process is compromised – if, for example, the mother is unresponsive, immersed in her own feelings rather than those of her child – an insecure attachment is formed. By the time the child is one year old it can be diagnosed as showing the characteristic patterns of insecurity – avoidant, confused, clinging and unavailable. This behaviour is a defensive response to parenting where the parent has put her own needs before her child's needs.

Over time, the insecure child develops a strong need to keep his mother happy and support her feelings. This represents the beginnings of a dysfunctional relationship, leading to an unhealthy emotional state for the child as it grows, with the possibility of it developing into narcissism or codependency by early adulthood.

A human child is totally dependent and at the mercy of other humans. From birth to their teenage years, human beings are almost entirely influenced by and dependent on their environment, which is usually controlled by their parents. So the physical and emotional growth of all newborn humans to the end of adolescence is largely dependent on their parents. Children use their parents as role-models and mimic their behaviour in later life, particularly in relation to emotional issues.

What happens when the parenting goes wrong? It went wrong in the cases of Adolf Hitler and Joseph Stalin; both had abusive fathers who also abused their mothers, so it is highly likely that both Hitler and Stalin were emotionally abused as children, and possibly also physically abused. As adults both were incredibly cunning and ruthlessly exploited people for their own ends, unashamedly enjoying and benefiting from the labour of others. They were malignant narcissists who started life with dysfunctional relationships with their parents and who sustained their dysfunctionality into adulthood.

It is widely accepted that Hitler and Stalin were exceptionally evil malignant narcissists, but the principle that narcissistic dysfunctionality begins early in life and through adolescence holds good. However, this book is not about the exceptional cases, although they often serve as good examples; it's about the large and growing number of narcissistic individuals in society who wreak havoc in the home, at work and socially on innocent and unsuspecting people through their inflated self-esteem, their lack of empathy for others, their feelings of entitlement to special treatment and privileges, their disagreeableness, and their all-consuming need for attention.

The symptoms displayed by narcissists are the means by which we can identify them. But don't think for a minute that such identification is easy. This book identifies all of the symptoms they display and portrays how many narcissists cause incalculable damage to the lives of their spouses, their children, their work colleagues and others. They often achieve high-powered positions in politics or industry, where their behaviour can have catastrophic effects. But when challenged, they always manage to move the blame onto others, using all of the psychological tactics at their disposal – denial, distortion, lying, and so on.

There is one large group of individuals who suffer at the hands of narcissists, but most of them do not even know it. They are codependents, or co-narcissists. This group of people are also victims of abuse during their childhood, usually being the children of one narcissistic parent and one codependent parent who used their children as repositories for their own emotional pain. These codependents have been groomed by their parents to always take the blame, so when they grow up they are attracted to narcissists as spouses, bosses and friends, as here they feel secure; their relationship with their narcissist mirrors the relationship that their parents had with each other. The narcissist-codependent parent combination is also the ideal combination for producing malignant narcissists.

This book looks at how narcissists and codependents interact, and analyses the words used by narcissists, and by codependents when directly influenced by their narcissistic controller. When a narcissist is disparaging someone he dislikes, if you look deeply enough, and know the narcissist well enough, you can always find the real meaning behind the words, which invariably relate to the narcissist's feelings of paranoia and envy. All malignant narcissists suffer from acute paranoia and pathological envy.

It also asks such questions as whether 'narcissists and codependents can find happiness', and it looks at what happiness is and how family behaviour can be changed to avoid producing the malignant narcissists and their codependent collaborators found in ever-increasing numbers in today's society.

There have been a lot of high-profile narcissists throughout history up to the present day. Hitler and Stalin were only two of the many narcissistic leaders who were responsible for the deaths of millions in the twentieth century. In the twenty-first century, we have already seen how narcissistic leaders such as Saddam Hussein in Iraq and Robert Mugabe in Zimbabwe can wreak havoc on their own subjects and others. Many will argue that other high-profile figures such as George W. Bush and Osama Bin Laden also qualify as narcissists.

It's not just politicians. Narcissistic business leaders have in recent times created spectacular crashes; there's little doubt that self-serving narcissistic behaviour by business leaders was behind the collapse of the giant oil company Enron, and also behind the failure of financial institutions that contributed to the wider 'credit crunch' that has more recently caused turmoil in industry and society across the globe.

These big events affect almost all of us, but we feel there is little or nothing that we can do to change things. Consequently, we just accept the status quo. But at a more personal level, there are many people who suffer havoc in the workplace wreaked upon them by narcissistic bosses; such individuals are caught between the desire to provide for their family and the alternative path of confrontation, which risks unemployment. Then there are the women who suffer in their own home, caught between the desire to escape from a nar-cissistic husband and the need to provide a home for their children. The vast majority of people, particularly in the western world, are either currently suffering at the hands of narcissists or have suffered at some time in the past, either in the home or in the workplace. But many don't even realise it.

The best way to alleviate this suffering is through disseminating the knowledge required for innocent, decent people to recognise those who are currently causing their suffering, and to recognise those who are likely to cause suffering in the future if given the opportunity. In a democratic society we can vote bad politicians out if we are sufficiently well informed to recognise them; we can change jobs to avoid a bad boss, or we can even ensure that he isn't pro-moted to a position of authority in the first place; and in the domestic situation we can avoid making a long-term commitment to a partner who will turn our lives into a nightmare once we are committed and it's too late. But that's only if we can recognise the narcissistic symptoms in the first place.

Success in western society today is often measured by how much money you make. While most people agree that having sufficient money is important, most people agree that money does not bring happiness. There would be less anxiety and stress in the world if people redefined success as being about identifying and achieving their goals and leading a good life, morally and ethically. This form of success would bring with it the very desirable side effect of happiness.

You can only achieve your goals in collaboration with others, so leadership skills and teamwork cannot be ignored. But the whole process will be sabotaged if you don't have the ability to recognise narcissism at work. For example, at the outset, a narcissistic spouse or boss may not − in fact, probably will not − have malevolent intentions towards you, but his (the majority of narcissists are male) personality problems will ultimately result in you giving up on your goals to pander to his emotional needs. Your dream of genuine fulfilment and happiness will just slip away, and you may not even know why.

This book addresses the inseparable topics of narcissism, leadership and teamwork. They are inseparable because narcissists always want to lead, but they are rarely the best leaders, and they are the antithesis of good team workers.

The narcissist will always put himself forward to lead a group or team, as he feels it is his right. If he isn't appointed as leader, he will snipe at the person who is, exaggerating any of his failures, large or small, and diminishing and undermining any of his successes, until the leader gets frustrated through not being recognised for his effort and achievements. No matter how genuine and successful the leader is, eventually he will get tired of the sniping; he will then stand down and let the narcissist take over.

So if you want to achieve your goals, lead a fulfilled life, and benefit from the very desirable by-product of happiness, a better understanding of these three topics – narcissism, leadership and teamwork – will enable you to avoid being emotionally trapped and to either take control of your life or, if preferred, allow someone who has your best interests at heart to share in the control of your life – an emotionally healthy husband or wife, for example.

1

What's the Problem?

Do You Understand What is Going On in Your Life?

'But, O, how bitter a thing it is to look into happiness through another man's eyes!'[1]

Have you ever been in a really good mood, chatting in a friendly manner to your partner, or to a colleague at work about an idea you have had? Something positive that will be of benefit not just to you, but to others as well. But your partner or work colleague responds cuttingly, 'What's it got to do with you? Keep your nose out.' You may then end up in an argument.

How did you end up arguing? You know that you have been reasonable, talking sense. You have no axe to grind, you were just putting forward an idea, a proposition, perhaps, that is of obvious benefit all round. Yet you walk away wondering how on earth a friendly chat about something so obviously beneficial has ended up in such acrimony.

It's natural to assume that you must have said something wrong, must have missed something so important that what seemed obviously helpful must actually be detrimental somehow. But what was it that you missed?

Or perhaps you have just caught him, or her, at a bad time. Of course, we all have our ups and downs. Everyone has moments when they aren't feeling so good, snap back at a friend or colleague, and then later regret it.

If it's a one-off encounter, it may be that you have just caught him or her at a bad moment. But if, first of all, it doesn't happen in your relationship with the other person at all, then it happens occasionally, and then you never know what to expect, there may be something more sinister behind the relationship – perhaps a power struggle. Eventually it reaches a stage when you feel that you don't even want to make any suggestions as you know that the response will be couched in emotional and aggressive terms – 'Leave it to me; you don't know what you are talking about. Remember …' – and they will then go on to identify something from the past that you did wrong. It may be something that you considered unimportant at the time so you have completely forgotten about it, but it is thrown back in your face.

The answer to the question about what it is that you have missed is most likely that you haven't missed anything. It's nothing to do with something you have missed, nor is it anything to do with the validity of your idea, nor is it anything to do with your logic, common sense or what's best. It's all to do with the other person's state of mind. And their behaviour is all to do with taking control over your relationship with them, forcing you to adapt your behaviour to accommodate theirs.

This behaviour is narcissism, and the adaptation of your behaviour to accommodate the narcissist is codependency.

But we are all narcissistic and codependent to some degree. When we feel our self-esteem going up or down in relation to how we perceive others think and feel about us, we are being narcissistic. When we feel that we are not living up to someone else's needs or expectations and we feel guilt or anxiety, we are being codependent.

So what differentiates the narcissist from a normal person who has feelings, sometimes anxious ones, sometimes upset ones, and sometimes angry ones? These are all emotions that we feel from time to time, primarily dependent upon the environment. We all care about what others think of us, don't we? Parents reprimand their children when they misbehave – so is this controlling behaviour, narcissism? Are we all narcissists, then?

To a degree, we are – but the fact is that normal parents reprimand their children so that they learn where boundaries lie, whereas narcissistic parents do so to establish emotional control over their offspring. A narcissist must be in control, or at least must feel that he is in control, at all times. Yes, we all care about what others think of us, but normal people don't live their lives by continually monitoring what others think and feel about them. Normal people don't react with aggression when they hear something that could be perceived by some as an ego threat. Normal people aren't paranoid and envious.

If it is a power struggle that you have identified, then it's a power struggle that you are going to lose. You cannot beat a narcissist, because a narcissist's survival depends entirely upon being in control, or at least upon having the perception of being in control. This includes controlling you if you are the marital or life partner, the business partner, the co-director, even the next-door neighbour.

Highly narcissistic people tend to be neurotic, paranoid and very, very envious. They compare themselves with everyone they meet. If they feel superior, it's a boost to their self-esteem, so they feel better. But when a narcissist encounters someone who is superior to them in some respect – for example, intellectually – and, perhaps more importantly, those around the narcissist know that that person is superior, the narcissist suffers a blow to his ego and reacts with anger and aggression.

So far it sounds remarkably easy to identify a narcissist, but nothing could be further from the truth. A narcissist doesn't show his anger and aggression in the way normal people do. Narcissists always have anger and aggression simmering just beneath the surface, but they quickly learn to control it. The narcissist is utilitarian and calculating so as to enable him to acquire power, which he needs to protect himself from others penetrating the mask that he puts up to prevent them from discovering his true self.

Because of his fear of exposure, the narcissist operates behind a façade of respectability and altruism, which he protects at all times.

But it cannot be overstated how much people underestimate the ability of the narcissist to deceive.

On the one hand, he presents himself as, perhaps, the perfect husband, caring, courteous, bringing gifts home after work; or as the perfect boss, helping his subordinates, giving big pay increases and generous time off. He is generally an all-round good citizen, sitting on the PTA committee, supporting the church and other causes, for example. Anyone who accuses such a considerate, often well-dressed professional of being scheming and immoral, and of behaving like an emotionally disturbed adolescent, will be accused either of lying or of being insanely envious of him.

On the other hand, if the narcissist becomes aware that someone has seen through his façade, that person will then see his vindictive and malicious nature, as the narcissist will take whatever actions are necessary to protect the false image that he projects. He will be careful not to expose the vindictive and malicious side of his nature to others; he'll restrict it solely to his victim. The only others who may be privy to his behaviour will be those codependents who have taken on his world view and who will therefore support his actions, by, for example, continual defamation, disparagement, belittling or character assassination of the victim.

The stock-in-trade of highly narcissistic people is self-aggrandisement and the denigration of others. But as the narcissist is acutely concerned with others' perceptions of him, he is careful to not appear boastful when indulging in self-aggrandisement. However, the denigration of others is an indulgence in which he can partake at any time. The person who is the object of the vilification is not normally present, but this is not a strict rule. If the object is codependent, under the control of the narcissist and not likely to answer back and thereby cause a blow to the narcissist's ego, then the object is considered by the narcissist to be fair game. This usually happens in the presence of others whom the narcissist feels a need to impress with his power and influence.

The length of time it takes to become codependent depends primarily on how codependent a person is at the start. Those at greatest risk will have been brought up by narcissistic parents, or by one narcissistic and one codependent parent, so they are predisposed to being controlled by narcissists.

But we already know that we are all narcissistic and codependent to some degree, so we all have the potential to become both narcissistic and codependent, don't we? Philip Zimbardo's Stanford University prison study[2] which took place in the summer of 1971 suggests that this is indeed the case.

Zimbardo and his fellow researchers had planned a two-week investigation into the psychology of prison life. College students were randomly assigned to be either guards or prisoners. But the study had to be stopped after only six days because of what was happening to the students. In only a few days, the guards adopted narcissistic behavioural characteristics. Their behaviour resulted in the prisoners becoming depressed and showing signs of extreme stress.

The students were an average group of healthy, intelligent middle-class males. They were arbitrarily divided into two groups by a flip of the coin. At the beginning of the study there were no differences between the students assigned to be prisoners and those assigned to be guards. But the different environments into which the students were placed had profound and contrasting effects on their behaviour.

Narcissists and codependents are just opposite sides of the same coin, so to speak; it depends on their environment, as the Stanford University prison study demonstrated. Even a highly narcissistic person who encounters a superior narcissist may behave in a codependent manner in his or her company. A primarily codependent person who finds himself in a position of power may become narcissistic. As Lord Acton said, 'Power tends to corrupt, and absolute power corrupts absolutely.'[3]

As narcissists and codependents have usually been brought up by one narcissistic and one codependent parent, they believe that all relationships require one to dominate and one to be subservient, and both narcissists and codependents can adopt either role when the environment demands it.

Only when narcissism and codependency interfere with our ability to enjoy our lives do they become a problem. We all engage in 'low-level' narcissism and codependency during our daily lives, but we don't usually notice this in ourselves or in others, as we acknowledge that the normal pressures involved in our day-to-day lives can cause both stress and anxiety as well as fun and laughter.

Stress is natural and may even be desirable. A degree of low-level narcissism can cause stress which, in turn, can make us perform better, make us more alert and help us in difficult situations. But stress is only good as a short-lived response. Too much stress or stress and anxiety over a long time can lead to illness and physical and emotional exhaustion, unhappiness, and worse.

It is thus important to be able to recognise narcissistic behaviour, both in yourself and in others, as its impact on you, your family members, your friends and your work colleagues can be devastating.

If you are narcissistic, deep down inside you may already be aware that you are. Perhaps you acknowledge your own neurotic, paranoid and envious behaviour, but through your own natural defences, primarily denial, you deal with it by avoiding thinking about it. You simply don't allow thoughts of failure or inadequacy to enter your mind, and you deal with your negative, envious behaviour towards others by justifying it, using other defences such as projection.[4] Reading this book may enable you to take the first step towards dealing with your narcissistic tendencies. The first step, possibly the most difficult, is to acknowledge that you have a problem.

If you are not narcissistic you may still recognise in others the behaviours described in this book – those of narcissism and of codependency. But at the same time you will also almost certainly recognise some of those same behavioural characteristics in yourself. We must not forget that we are all narcissistic and codependent to some degree.

It is also important to understand where, when and how narcissism occurs. The conditions that foster narcissism and codependency behaviours aren't always in prisons, although Philip Zimbardo's Stanford University prison study gives us a clear insight into how even normal, decent people can behave narcissistically given suitable environmental conditions. Narcissism and codependency can be found in almost all environments – for example, in the home, in the workplace and in social settings.

The following points need to be considered if we are going to understand narcissism and how to remove, or at least reduce, its destructive influence: it's essential to recognise narcissistic characteristics, such as those exhibited by the manager obsessed with power and control; it's also important to know what the underlying causes of narcissism are – whether, for example, it can be traced back to the parents. At work, you need to know how to manage a narcissist as part of your team; equally vital are the questions of whether there are differences between narcissistic men and narcissistic women, and whether you are controlled by a narcissist, at home or at work.

There are other questions in the work environment that may need to be answered regarding narcissists' abilities as leaders, how businesses run by narcissists fair, and what mechanisms narcissists use to influence other team members. Their ability to influence other team members will also extend to their home environment.

Understanding narcissism and codependency can be the first step in ameliorating narcissistic relationships, either from the narcissist's side or as experienced by the codependent. Better understanding may lead to less stress on both sides. If this book helps to reduce any amount of stress and anxiety in the home or in the workplace, then writing it will have been worthwhile.

Of course, the ideal situation would be to swap narcissism or codependency for happiness – real happiness, not that fleeting feeling of gratification when you have maligned someone who has said something to hurt your ego, or that brief moment of pleasure when someone compliments your new car or your new hairstyle, but an underlying, almost permanent feeling of contentment, combined with the ability to take knocks without feeling the need to respond.

Can this be achieved? Is there some way for the narcissist to be happy other than through the use of self-aggrandisement and the denigration of others? For the narcissist, however, where will the boosts to their self-esteem come from without disparaging their partner or their work colleague? In fact, for them, doesn't high self-esteem equate to happiness?

Narcissists always seem to claim to be happy when asked, so it appears that, for them, self-aggrandisement and the denigration of others is a strategy that works. But we must not forget that narcissists and codependents use lies and distortion of fact in the same way that murderers would do in court when trying to save themselves from the gallows. There are similarities between the two situations: the logic that the the narcissist uses is very much the same logic that applies to the murderer. Both believe that their very survival depends upon what they say next. In the case of the murderer, perhaps it is literally his very survival that is at stake; in the case of the narcissist, it is the protection of the (false) image, the mask that he is projecting, that he is in danger of losing. At virtually any cost, he doesn't want anyone to get under his veneer, see behind his mask and find out the truth – that his 'image' is his only protection of his extremely fragile ego. Protection of his ego is absolutely paramount in his eyes.

However, if we are all narcissistic or codependent to some degree, is there in fact any way to achieve real happiness? What about those of us who are highly narcissistic? This book also attempts to deal with the thorny problem of how moral and ethical behaviour relates to narcissism.

Moral and ethical behaviour is something that highly narcissistic people have most likely not practised, at least since reaching adulthood. But this doesn't mean that highly narcissistic people don't understand what moral and ethical behaviour is. It is simply a question of priorities. The highly practised automatic defence mechanisms associated with both narcissism and codependency can come into play in every situation where the ego is threatened, and this may simply mean confronting any non-routine situation with denial, distortion of facts and projection, which are used without any concern for the morality or ethicality of the behaviour, as the priority is the protection of the false image or ego.

Of course, narcissism and codependency can be viewed from an entirely different perspective. The two conditions may be considered to be the natural way of things. Narcissism appears to have been rampant in the past – think, for example, of King Henry VIII – and many consider it to be so today. And, along with narcissism, there is always codependency. The two go hand in hand.

So maybe there is no reason why narcissistic behaviour should not be considered acceptable. If it is so prevalent in today's society, should it be accepted as the norm? Or are the anxiety, stress, and emotional pain and suffering it causes too big a burden to bear?

Typical narcissistic personalities have grown into adulthood with admiring parents, but without sufficient guidance from them, without knowing where interpersonal boundaries lie, and without having to look after themselves. So they need someone to take the place of their parents, to admire them and to look after them.

Typical codependents, on the other hand, have grown into adulthood with over-controlling parents whom they have been taught to admire and run around after, while having to endure the typical narcissistic parent's vilification during their childhood years, with such scalding comments as: 'You're useless!' 'You're a waste of space!' 'Give it to me, I'll show you how to do it!' 'Don't ever do that again!' 'Why do I always have to do everything for you?' In fact, they have learned from their narcissistic parent exactly how to behave in the company of a narcissist. Consequently, the narcissistic person-ality and the codependent personality fit together very well.

Does the problem lie primarily with the codependent mother who failed to protect the child while her narcissistic husband took out his aggression on the child? Is it morally right for the codependent to look on while a fellow human being is being belittled, treated like dirt by the narcissist, without doing anything to prevent it? In fact, it is usually the case that, over time, the codependent (be it the mother or the father who is the codependent onlooker) takes on the char-acteristics of the narcissist, viewing the world in the same distorted way that the narcissist does, and in so doing supports the narcissist's behaviour.

There are extreme examples that are reported in the media from time to time where a mother is implicated in the death of her child by severe neglect. Invariably, there is also a pathologically envious stepfather or boyfriend involved who, over time, dehumanises the child in the eyes of the mother, paving the way for the neglect to take place. Pathological envy is the hallmark of a severely narcissistic individual.

It may be that narcissism, and its aspirant cousin codependency, need to have an injection of moral and ethical behaviour. Aristotle believed that man will always make the right decision if he is in possession of all of the facts and has sufficient knowledge. This book may be part of the process involved in imparting the facts and knowledge required for those with narcissistic and codependent traits to make the right decisions in life, both morally and ethically.

2

Narcissism

Are You Neurotic, Paranoid or Narcissistic?

Neurotics, paranoiacs and narcissists are surprisingly common in the home, and in management, where they are often leaders.

Human beings are social creatures and need social interaction, feedback, and validation of their worth. Emotionally mature individuals don't need to go hunting for these; they gain it naturally from their daily life, especially from stable relationships at home and from their work. The emotionally immature person, however, has a low level of self-esteem[1] and therefore often feels inferior. This can lead to neurosis,[2] paranoia[3] and narcissism.[4]

When asked how many business leaders are well-adjusted individuals, Manfred Kets de Vries, an internationally recognised expert on leadership and organisational behaviour, replied, 'You can argue that 20 per cent of the general population is relatively healthy; 20 per cent is relatively sick; and the other 60 per cent, who all suffer from "neurotic misery", are somewhere in the middle. That applies to most people I meet.'[5]

Alfred Adler[6] believed that feeling inferior is a neurosis. The neurotic person becomes insecure, indecisive, compliant, and so on. He begins to rely on people to carry him along, even manipulating them into supporting him. To counter these feelings of insecurity, some will spend a large proportion of their lives creating situations in which they become the centre of attention.

18

Another way that people respond to feeling inferior is to develop a superiority complex. This involves covering up their feeling of inferiority by pretending to be superior. If you feel small, one way to feel big is to make others feel smaller. Bullies operate in this way. Other examples are those who put others down for their gender, race, ethnic origins, religious beliefs, sexual orientation, weight, height, etc.

A neurotic person may also suffer from paranoia. A 'paranoid personality disorder' is a pattern of pervasive distrust and suspicion of others such that their motives are interpreted as malevolent. An inability to trust, doubts about the loyalty of others, distortion and fabrication, misinterpretation, and bearing grudges unnecessarily are hallmarks of the disorder. Pathological envy,[7] instinctive aggressive counterattack, the need to control others, and the gathering of trivial or circumstantial 'evidence' to support the envious beliefs also feature.

A paranoid person may also be a narcissist. The need for attention is paramount to the person with 'narcissistic personality disorder', and they will do almost anything to obtain it.

Narcissists are characterised by a persistent pattern of grandiosity and self-importance, a need for admiration, and a lack of empathy. They overestimate their abilities and inflate their achievements, often appearing boastful and pretentious, whilst correspondingly underestimating and devaluing the achievements and accomplishments of others.[8] Pathological narcissism is a result of faulty self-development and results in the maladaptive use of interpersonal relations to promote self-expression.

The narcissist craves admiration. He ceaselessly works to appear important and interesting and to be the centre of attention. His craving for attention and admiration is never-ending, constantly seeking sources of supply. But when the narcissist detects someone who doesn't admire him, or who doesn't acknowledge the importance he attaches to himself, he reacts with hostility or disparagement.

However, the narcissist is not alone. He needs a partner, both at home and at work; a codependent.[9] The codependent partner will be a follower, not a leader, and a provider of admiration. Although the narcissist may inflict mental cruelty and humiliation on his partner, the two of them support each other's neurotic behaviour. The partner usually craves and encourages his narcissistic friend's paranoid, or even threatening, attention. She (or he) becomes accommodating and understanding, caring for the whims and mood swings of the narcissist, eventually learning to adapt to the narcissist's world view. Her behaviour and reactive patterns tend to reinforce the narcissist's behaviour. The narcissist uses this partner as an anchor, a 'trusted sidekick', and feels that she is an extension of himself.

At home, the narcissistic husband's continual need for attention and the undermining of his wife's position (the majority of narcissists are male, as already noted)[10] through his constant denigration of her, which may be in front of the children, eventually turns his wife's life to one of spending all her time trying to please her narcissistic master, not inflaming his temper so as to avoid chastisement or embarrassment.

At work, the narcissist's continual need for attention tends to impact on his job, and this becomes obvious to his work colleagues, who naturally look to the narcissist's codependent partner to do something about it. This allows the partner to assume a superior position and to treat the narcissist as his or her 'patient' who is in need of care. This presumed status endows codependent partners with authority and provides them with a way to distance themselves from their own emotions (and from the narcissist's). Narcissists' partners are permanently enmeshed in battles to prove themselves as worthwhile (both to the ever-critical and humiliating narcissist and to themselves).[11]

The nature of the narcissist in the work environment is such that he will not be satisfied until he has manipulated himself to the top of the organisation. But a narcissistic leader is not capable of putting the organisation's needs before his personal needs. The result is likely to be at best a roller-coaster ride for the organisation.

Can You Recognise a Narcissist?

At home, the narcissist is not capable of putting his family's needs before his own. At work, the narcissist is not capable of putting the organisation's needs before his own.[12]

It is difficult to recognise a narcissist because he (or she) spends all of his time acting, protecting his ego by presenting to the world a false image. Consequently, he becomes a master of deceit. Nevertheless, it is particularly important to be able to recognise someone who has the potential to make a significant negative long-term impact on your life. In the home, the narcissist has the capability of destroying a marriage and family life. In the workplace, his behaviour can be damaging to his organisation's performance.

If you are the victim, the narcissist will play upon your codependent vulnerability, which we all have to some extent. He will put you at the centre of your relationship with him; you will be the focal point, with everything revolving around you. This is the process of 'hooking' you, although he doesn't see it this way. His only interest is to impress you so that you continue to admire him. Admiration is the boost to his self-esteem that he continually craves.

The process of hooking you is carried out by doing everything for you (as his parents did for him); if he is your boyfriend, he'll be your knight in shining armour – he'll protect you, be at your side at every opportunity, impressing your family, friends and work colleagues; nothing is too much to ask of him.

You enjoy being the centre of attention. Any codependency in you will have been brought about by the controlling behaviour of your narcissistic parent, so to meet someone who is willing to put you at the centre without asking for anything in return is everything you want. The only hint of his controlling behaviour, which he is in effect hiding from you, will be his constant probing into your personal affairs – always for your benefit, of course.

For example, he may suggest to you that he can get you a better deal for your mobile phone; he will arrange to get your car serviced for a better price; he will arrange a better television deal; he may show you where best to invest your money; if you have difficulty affording something, he'll pay for you – the list is endless. Any way of entangling himself into your affairs, he will find. This makes your later escape all the more difficult.

The narcissist has now prepared you for manipulation through emotional attacks that will inevitably come; it is only a matter of time. Because there was an element of narcissistic behaviour on your side at the beginning, you will feel unable to defend yourself against the attacks. His accusations are simply projections of his own narcissistic feelings, but as there is an element of truth in them – you were completely happy to be at the centre of attention when he put you there – doubt creeps in. You ask yourself, 'How can someone I admire so much be wrong?' And your answer will be, 'It must be me.' So you lose the argument. And you continue losing arguments thereafter.

An argument with a narcissist can begin with something so trivial that you will wonder how it was possible to start it in the first place. The following is an argument between Pete, a narcissist, and Bethany, after Pete had forgotten to pick up milk from the shop whilst Bethany was at work, as agreed that morning between the two of them:

Bethany: Did you get the milk?

Pete: We don't need milk because we're having wine with dinner.

Bethany: We do need milk. Will you go and get some milk from the shop, please?

Pete: Stop nagging me.

Bethany: I'm not nagging you. I'm just asking if you can get some milk from the shop. We have run out and I'm cooking us a meal and I need milk for the rice pudding. In any case, we will need some in the morning for breakfast.

Pete: You really know how to get on people's nerves, don't you? You always do that. You're impossible to get on with. I never get any time to myself.

Bethany: Always do what?

Pete: You get on my nerves; you always have something to moan about.

Bethany: Why do I get on your nerves? I only asked you to go to the shop and get some milk.

Pete: You get on my nerves because you're always opening your big fat mouth and moaning. Moan, moan, moan, that's all I ever hear.

Bethany: No I don't.

Pete: Yes you do. You moaned at me last week when you wanted me to clean up that mess.

Bethany: Well you made it.

Pete: I was doing the job for *you*.

And so the argument goes on. What is apparent very quickly in arguing with a narcissist is that the facts are completely immaterial. The substantive matter – that there is a need for milk and that Pete is best situated to go and get it – is entirely irrelevant.

What really matters to Pete is the avoidance of blame. It was Pete who was at fault – he forgot the pick up the milk earlier. But he adopts a typically narcissistic strategy of not admitting that he was at fault and causing an argument as a distraction. When Bethany is not immediately drawn away from the question of going to get some milk, Pete resorts to getting personal – '... you're always opening your big fat mouth and moaning' – in order to raise the emotional stakes and draw Bethany into an unrelated, personal issue. Bethany is now concerned with defending herself from Pete's personal attack on her.

Thus Pete has succeeded in converting the conversation into an argument and moving the dialogue away from his failure to pick up the milk, so avoiding any risk of accepting blame. At the same time he has avoided being told what to do – again, something that narcissists detest.

Pete's emotional response to failure is to feel shame, which he feels must be avoided at almost any cost. Being accused of failure, being blamed and so being made to feel ashamed – this most probably relates back to the way he was treated as a child when he failed to live up to his parents' expectations. It is not the importance of the 'failure' that matters to the narcissist – in this case, forgetting to pick up milk is a most trivial failure in most people's eyes; what matters to him is the trigger of being reminded of painful repressed feelings from his childhood, fed into his consciousness from the unconscious part of his mind. And Bethany's request – '. . . will you go and get some milk from the shop, please?' – despite being accompanied by 'please', triggers further repressed painful feelings from Pete's childhood of being told by his parents what to do, probably at an age when he needed to be allowed to make decisions for himself, but was not allowed to do so.

You will only win an argument against a narcissist when you first meet him and he is trying to impress you, or much later on, when you are completely under his control. If you get so weak that you can't look after him, he'll manipulate your emotional state so that you are able to look after him, but he'll never let you get sufficiently strong to be able to stand up to him, or to run away.

The narcissist's behaviour in the workplace is similar to his behaviour at home, but the two are complementary in some ways. If he can get the admiration that he so craves in one environment, he may be easier to please in the other. This aspect of his behaviour makes it so much more difficult to recognise the narcissist.

He will inevitably use the two environments – home and work – to his own ends. He can garner admiration from his wife or lover by embellishing his position and exploits at work, and he can garner admiration from his colleagues at work by embellishing his relationships and exploits in his private life. Lies and distortion of fact come naturally, but the two can also impact on each other in different ways. Difficulties at work may be transferred to the home environment, and the family may suffer. Equally, difficulties at home may be transferred to the workplace, where colleagues or subordinates may have to endure his wrath. Problems at home or at work are usually born out of the narcissist's paranoia or envy, which surface with little or no provocation.

Researchers have found that narcissists react much more emotionally than non-narcissists, sometimes with 'narcissistic rage'[13] when their self-esteem or ego is threatened.[14] Social comparison information is especially influential in terms of a narcisist's mood and self-esteem fluctuations, as he processes social information in terms of its relevance to the self – that is, he reacts to negative feedback with more anger and aggression and with lower self-esteem than a non-narcissist does. 'Overall, individuals high in narcissism displayed amplified responses to social comparison information, experiencing greater positive effect from downward comparisons and greater hostile effect from upward comparisons.'[15]

For example, it has been recognised for some time that narcissists prize intellectual performance above almost everything else,[16] so a better-educated or better-qualified work colleague would likely evoke a hostile response through upward comparison.

Because of a propensity to internalise failure, the narcissist's emotional response to failure is to feel shame, as opposed to the guilt typically felt by non-narcissists. So in order to avoid shame, which the narcissist feels must be done at all costs, he externalises blame for negative events.[17] As he feels someone must be guilty, he almost always attributes blame to others. Only when his self-esteem is particularly high, perhaps through some positive feedback he has engineered, does he accept blame, and only then if it can be seen as a magnanimous gesture.

A narcissist is someone who is overtly or subtly arrogant, exhibitionistic, vain, manipulative, and greedy for admiration.[18] Narcissistic rage, character assassination[19] and projection[20] are some of the overt ways in which the narcissist expresses him or herself. For example, she may envy a work colleague's beauty, and project her feelings onto her colleague by accusing her of being envious.

The denial of remorse and of gratitude are two of the more subtle ways used to protect an internal sense of grandiosity. An example of a narcissist's ability to be subtle might be when he arrives late for a meeting. Rather than offer a sincere apology, he may blame someone else for keeping him talking, thus externalising the fault ('It's not my fault') and maintaining his sense of grandiosity ('It's because I'm so important that everyone wants to keep me talking').

Despite tending to be exhibitionistic, it is very rare to hear a narcissist brag or boast. Instead, he tends to 'drop' information in the form of an ostensibly ordinary matter-of-fact report, which appears to be intended to elicit admiration without asking for it. For example, rather than say, 'I was so please to meet our CEO, Peter Smith', he will casually allude to '. . . lunch with Peter', in a way that induces a sense of distance and inferiority in the recipient of the information; again maintaining his sense of grandiosity.[21]

A distinction must be made between 'normal' or 'healthy' narcissism on the one hand and 'malignant' or 'pathological' narcissism on the other. We all have some degree and variety of narcissistic delusion which, if it is not too great, is normal and healthy. But the pathological narcissist has a level of delusion that is divorced from reality.[22]

Kernberg used a theoretical frame to differentiate between 'normal' and 'pathological' narcissism, combining ego psychology[23] and object relations[24] theory. Normal narcissism refers to well-integrated representations of the self and others, whilst pathological narcissism relates to an impaired intra-psychic structure, with grandiose self-representation and a severe pathology in object relations.[25]

Lubit[26] compared 'healthy' and 'destructive' narcissism in relation to their long-term impact on organisations, but his analysis of the characteristics of the two very different types of narcissism can equally be applied to narcissists' behaviour in other walks of life.

With regard to self-confidence, Lubit describes the healthy narcissist as having high outward self-confidence in line with reality, whereas the destructive narcissist is simply grandiose. He found that the healthy narcissist may enjoy power, but the destructive narcissist pursues power at all costs, and lacks normal inhibitions in its pursuit. In relationships, he found that the healthy narcissist has real concern for others and their ideas and does not exploit or devalue others, whereas the destructive narcissist's concerns are limited to expressing socially appropriate responses when convenient, and with devaluing and exploiting others without remorse.

When Lubit looked at their ability to follow a consistent path, he found that the healthy narcissist has values and follows through on plans, whereas the destructive narcissist lacks values, is easily bored and often changes course. It was a similar story when he looked at the narcissist's roots, or foundations. The healthy narcissist had enjoyed a healthy childhood with support for self-esteem and appropriate limits on behaviour towards others, whereas the destructive narcissist had endured a traumatic childhood, which had the effect of undercutting his true sense of self-esteem, resulting in him learning that he doesn't need to be considerate of others.

It is rare for a narcissistic individual to be diagnosed with Narcissistic Personality Disorder because those who really should be don't seek help and so don't get clinically assessed; it is usually members of their family or work colleagues who seek help to cope with them.

Here are a few pointers that may help you identify someone with this disorder:

- They lack empathy, and this colours everything they do. They may say 'How are you?' when you meet, but they are working from memory. They are not interested in how you are.
- Virtually all of their ideas or ways of behaving in a given situation are taken from others – from people they know and perhaps think of as an authority (this is know as 'mirroring').[27]
- Their sense of self-importance and lack of empathy means that they will often interrupt the conversations of others.
- They expect others to do the day-to-day chores as they feel too important to waste their time on common things.
- They constantly use 'I', 'me' and 'my' when they talk.
- They very rarely talk about their inner life – for example, their memories and dreams.
- They feel that the rules at work don't apply to them.

- They will always cheat whenever they think they can get away with it.
- If you share the workload with them, expect to do the lion's share yourself.
- They love to delegate work, and then interfere by micro-managing it. If it goes well, they take the credit; if it goes badly, they blame the person they delegated it to.
- There tend to be higher levels of stress with people who work with or interact with a narcissist, which in turn increases absenteeism and staff turnover.
- They get impatient and restless when the topic of discussion is about someone else, and not about them.

There are many other behavioural characteristics exhibited by the narcissist. There is a quick test for narcissism at the end of this book that you might wish to take.

One way to recognise a narcissist is to trust in your own intuition. As Sam Vaknin, a self-confessed narcissist, put it, 'One feels ill at ease in the presence of a narcissist for no apparent reason. No matter how charming, intelligent, thought provoking, outgoing, easy going and social the narcissist is – he fails to secure the sympathy of others, a sympathy he is never ready, willing, or able to reciprocate.'[28]

How Does Narcissism Occur in the Workplace?

Corporate narcissism is spreading with epidemic proportions throughout the business world.[29]

What links patrimonial bureaucracy and totalitarian organisations? The answer is narcissism. Narcissism in this case includes the narcissists and the codependents within their sphere of influence. Patrimonial bureaucracy occurs when codependent employees become personally loyal to their narcissistic superiors in such a way as to always feel the need to seek their approval before acting.

Narcissists foster this type of behaviour in all of their subordinates, and in all of their peers if possible, in order to develop their codependency. This works well for the narcissist's self-esteem, but not so well for the business. Narcissism in the workplace results in poor judgements that turn into costly decisions,[30] ultimately resulting in negative long-term outcomes.[31] As patrimonial bureaucracy spreads throughout the business, it becomes a totalitarian organisation.

Corporate narcissism occurs when a narcissist becomes the leader (CEO) or a member of the senior management team and gathers an adequate mix of codependents around him to support his narcissistic behaviour. This leads almost inevitably to deterioration in the organisation's performance. Narcissists profess company loyalty but are only really committed to their own agendas; thus, organisational decisions are founded on the narcissist's own interests rather than the interests of the organisation as a whole, those of the various stakeholders, or those of the environment in which the organisation operates.[32]

There have been many examples of corporate narcissism in industry over recent years. The collapse of the Houston energy company Enron in 2001 relates directly to the leadership of its CEO Jeff Skilling, appointed in 1996. In his book *Pipe Dreams: Greed, Ego, and the Death of Enron*, Robert Bryce stated: 'Enron failed because its leadership was morally, ethically and financially corrupt.' Skilling's leadership was critical in generating an organisational culture that mirrored narcissism, with its encouragement of blithe risk-taking, its mercenary approach to profit-making and its win-at-all costs attitude.

The failure of the Royal Bank of Scotland (RBS) in 2008 in the UK, which necessitated a takeover by the taxpayers in the guise of the British government to avoid complete collapse, can also be traced directly to narcissistic leadership. Sir Fred Goodwin built RBS into a powerhouse, ruthlessly exploiting a benevolent economic environment; but in an apparently narcissistic drive to take over a Dutch bank, ABN Amro, he also adopted blithe risk-taking behaviour. By refusing to back out of a high-risk deal when economic conditions deteriorated, he crashed in spectacular fashion, taking a once proud and great bank with him. In 2009, shortly after the departure of Sir Fred Goodwin, RBS announced the largest annual loss in UK corporate history.

Narcissism relates back to Greek mythology; Narcissus was a handsome young boy who fell in love with his own reflection, then died of starvation by confusing that reflection with his true self. Thus narcissists are addicted to their own image, constantly manipulating others to validate that image, and endlessly searching for the attainment of an idealised self, which, of course, cannot be achieved. In other words, narcissists rely on manipulating work and social relationships to support a self that cannot internally sustain a sense of well-being.

Thus, the narcissist can't succeed without codependents. If the narcissistic personality trait is to be activated, then the narcissist needs to be exposed to trait-relevant situational cues.[33] It is codependents, who do whatever the narcissist needs, sometimes working beyond healthy (and sometimes ethical) limits, who supply these cues. Narcissists and codependents are attracted to each other because narcissists crave power and codependents crave security.[34]

A narcissist can be described in terms of a bipolar self that has two poles or dimensions. In early life, one pole involves an immature grandiosity or a confident self-superiority that can develop into adult forms of ambitiousness. The other pole is associated with tendencies to idealise or admire the superiorities of others, and those tendencies can mature into an internalised system of ideals.[35] Narcissistic Personality Disorder represents an arrest in the development of healthy self-esteem.[36]

Parental nurturance, or good parenting, is therefore critical in the transformation of normal narcissistic traits into mature ambitions and ideals;[37] and parental nurturance predicts healthy self-esteem.[38] It isn't surprising, therefore, that when you look into the parental relationships of narcissists and codependents, you find problems, caused typically by the combination of one narcissistic parent and one codependent parent who singularly fails to stand up to her narcissistic partner.

If you identify someone in your workplace who you think has narcissistic characteristics, check their behaviour against the pointers given in this book, and look for their codependents, those do the narcissist's bidding and seek their approval before acting.

Is the Narcissistic Personality Obsessed with Power and Control?

The narcissist is addicted to power and control, without which he feels exposed to his real feelings of inferiority, inadequacy and worthlessness.

The narcissistic personality manifests itself in the narcissist's behaviour. He (or she) will seek to dominate every individual and every group with which he interacts, at home, socially and at work. Narcissism occurs in the workplace at almost every organisation, usually at or near to the top.[39] The narcissistic personality and its obsessive desire for control is not about control just for control's sake, but is an essential defence against the risk of receiving a narcissistic injury – a blow to the ego or self-esteem. The narcissistic personality has a defence mechanism that works incessantly to prevent others reminding the narcissist of his feelings of inferiority, inadequacy and worthlessness, which lower his self-esteem.

As Dr Bruce Gregory stated, 'many people have the fantasy that if they try hard, "do it right", be reasonable, logical, and have goodwill and a team approach, these factors will generate a positive outcome in interpersonal or group settings. This is about as deep a fantasy as one could possibly have, as it is not based in reality. Why is this? It is ... because a narcissist's survival is dependent upon having control, or the perception of control.'[40] When this control is challenged, he feels threatened and responds as though his very survival is at stake.

Over time, a narcissist will create an emotionally hazardous work environment for the non-narcissist. He will surround himself with codependents. If he is high enough up the organisation, he will appoint them. If he can't appoint them, he will make life so difficult for those who don't subscribe to his world view, or who don't tacitly accept it, that they will leave. The narcissist will eventually end up surrounded by individuals who play the pathological reciprocal role that his behaviour typically induces.

A huge problem in the work environment is that the codependents completely fail to recognise the narcissist's pathological behaviour. As they already subscribe to his world view, the codependents are already conditioned to accepting the narcissist's behaviour, and as Bruce Gregory stated, 'It is a well known dynamic in most psychological circles that if one is denying or cut off from an aspect of the self, it is very difficult ... to recognize this aspect in others.'[41]

But since the narcissist's defence system works incessantly to prevent others reminding him of his feelings of inferiority, inadequacy and worthlessness, and thus from lowering his self-esteem, how does he avoid situations occurring whereby his codependents cause this to happen, even inadvertently? Daniel Sankowsky described how this problem is avoided by both the narcissist leader and his codependents:

> ... under conditions of threat (which can simply mean confronting any non-routine situation), followers and leaders alike act on the basis of certain fundamental values, such as control of the encounter and avoidance of negative feelings, and also on the basis of strategies such as concealing thoughts and feelings, advocating fixed positions, unilaterally saving face, and sending mixed messages. Each side proceeds according to these values and strategies and assumes the other is doing the same. Both sides tacitly 'agree' not to discuss any of this.[42]

If the leader (CEO) has a narcissistic personality, he will make sure that his management team is composed of individuals with codependent characteristics. If the leader is codependent, and there is a narcissist in his management team, then the codependent will do the bidding of the narcissist (remember, he already subscribes to the narcissist's world view). The best bet for an effective leader is one who is a non-narcissist who has the strength of character to deal with narcissists.

But non-narcissists in the workplace who are committed to being fair and nice to others may further compound the problem. They are naturally unwilling or unprepared to hold the narcissist accountable for his behaviour. Confrontation is not part of their personality, so their failure to face up to the narcissist only serves to reinforce the narcissist's belief in his dominance, thereby strengthening his position.

An emotionally hazardous home or work environment is a house or workplace led by a narcissist who believes in demonstrating power and control over those around him, his family, or his employees, dominating them through a combination of direct threats and stealth methods. But when the narcissist gets his feelings hurt, or perceives that he has been slighted in any way, or is threatened by the fact that someone else's abilities might be better than his own, he will react with aggression. The time it takes for the narcissist to change from Mr Nice Guy to Mr Angry can be very short, and some of the methods he uses as means of control are abuse, narcissistic rage, splitting,[43] projection, character assassination, and intimidation.

At work the stealth methods used by narcissistic leaders and managers can create emotional turmoil for those around them. Name calling, talking down to employees, sexual harassment, disinformation, and using the silent treatment for those who have slighted him are just some examples of the subtle controlling techniques that gradually but consistently erode a normal workplace into one that is cancerous. And just as with cancer in the body, it can spread its malignancy throughout the organisation.[44]

In the home, the narcissist uses the same subtle controlling techniques to the same effect. A happy home will gradually but consistently erode into one where the narcissist's partner or spouse and their children always have to carefully select their words so as to not incur the wrath of the narcissist, who systematically suppresses the free expression of thought.

What Causes Narcissism?

'Sufficient unto himself, he becomes more and more self-absorbed – either hyper-vulnerable to every slight or brutally bullying his way to the "top" whose twin peaks are his own self-aggrandisement and the denigration of others.'[45]

Narcissism occurs as a result of low self-esteem, or of feeling inferior in certain situations, caused by a gap between the ideal self (whose standards are set by others – for example, parents) and the real self; this results in threatening situations (real or perceived), which lead to anxiety, which in turn lead to the development of defence mechanisms to defend the individual's ego. Defence against a real or perceived threat involves denial and distortion of facts, projection and splitting.

The hallmark of a narcissist is the development of a superiority complex as a response to feeling inferior. This involves exaggerating his own achievements and putting down anyone he perceives as a threat.

Narcissistic traits are quite common in adolescence, but this does not necessarily mean that the child will go on to become a narcissist. Research has found the diagnosis of narcissism to be significantly more common among men.[46] Faulty or inadequate parenting – for example, a lack of limit setting – is believed to be a major cause, and both permissive and authoritarian styles of parenting have been found to promote narcissistic symptoms. The following parenting behaviours may result in a child becoming a narcissist in adulthood:

- Permissive parents who give excessive praise to the child, thus fostering an unrealistic view of themselves[47]

- Overindulgence and spoiling[48]
- Failing to impose adequate discipline[49]
- Idealisation of the child[50]

Idealisation may require the child to suppress his or her own self-expression to meet the desires of the parent and to gain their love and approval.[51] To develop a realistic image of the self, the child must be provided with realistic information about discipline, and reasonable limits must be set by the parents as to what the child can and cannot do. Narcissists generally feel unprepared for adulthood, having been imbued with an unrealistic view of life.[52]

Narcissists are concerned with their image rather than with their selves. They often act to promote their image at the expense of their self.[53] The narcissistic self is a bipolar structure with the two extremes, consisting of an immature grandiosity at one end and a dependent over-idealisation of other people at the opposite end. Healthy self-esteem is not formed if a child is not valued for his or her own self-worth. Usually, the child is only used for the benefit of the parent's self-esteem and to further the parent's needs. A narcissistic personality may be formed to make up for this lack of support and encouragement from parents.[54]

The natural narcissistic tendencies in children during adolescence can cause parents to behave either in an authoritarian way or in a permissive way towards their child. This narcissistic vulnerability in adolescence makes the child prone to embarrassment and shame, self-consciousness and shyness, and questions of self-esteem and self-worth.[55] Healthy development of the self requires parenting that is demanding enough to encourage growth and independence but not so demanding as to prevent growth through over-control. Both extremes – a lack of guidance (permissiveness), and over-control (authoritarianism) – should be avoided to reduce the likelihood of the adolescent becoming a narcissist in adulthood.[56]

Many people, including many psychologists, believe that narcissism is a product of our times and our system of values.[57] The western world in particular is constantly bombarded by images of the ideal through the media, and this may contribute to the rapid growth of narcissism in society.

How Do You Manage a Narcissistic Team Member?

'It is a peculiarity of the paranoid universe, a grim face full of terrifying figures which paralyses all development ...' [58]

You have a team where members are focused on a joint goal or product, such as a presentation, completing in-class exercises, taking notes, writing a report, or creating a new design or prototype; it may be a senior management team such as a board of directors. It has the right balance of personality types and a leader with the right characteristics to ensure that the goal or goals of the team will be achieved. But you have a narcissist in the team whose increasing amount of negative influence is preventing the team from achieving its goals, or its full potential. So how do you deal with the narcissist?

Narcissistic Personality Disorder[59] and paranoia are closely linked, as both are with pathological envy.[60] The paranoia that the narcissist suffers leads to a fear of failure, resulting in impairment of his development.

This fear of failure, paranoia and pathological envy felt by the narcissist will ultimately result in him becoming a burden to the team. Eventually the narcissist's well-documented negative impact on co-workers or team members will take its toll.[61]

Narcissists are highly motivated, energetic, assertive and competitive. These characteristics relate closely to the 'Belbin' team role of Shaper,[62] a leadership team role. However, the potential benefits of the narcissist's leadership characteristics are lost through his narcissism. As Dr Roy Lubit explained, 'At the same time that [narcissistic] personality traits may help managers rise within an organisation, these same traits impair their ability to lead effectively';[63] and as Dr Belbin stated, 'The only option is the effective leader.'[64] We'll look in more detail at effective leadership in chapter 4.

It seems almost inevitable these days that there will be some personality disorders in a senior management team.[65] Unfortunately, in the case of narcissism, there is little that the leader or other team members can do for the narcissist as the likelihood of change in his personality is slim. As Ronningstam and Gunderson put it, 'For clinicians, the assiduous and sustained resistance to change common in patients with narcissistic personality disorder (NPD) has been especially noticeable and trying.'[66]

A commonsense approach to the problems caused by the narcissist would be to challenge him by pointing out his behavioural problems and the negative influence they are having on the team, but this would certainly invoke immediate denial, probably combined with distortion of facts. The narcissist would simply deny any wrongdoing and twist what was said or done so as to remove any guilt attributable to him, more often than not blaming any failures on another team member instead. In effect, narcissists will rewrite history, in such a way, as Theodore Millon put it, as 'to freely transform failures into successes, and to construct lengthy and intricate rationalizations that inflate their self-worth or justify what they believe is their right'.[67] Theodore Millon and Roger Davis further pointed out that narcissists 'remember the past as they would have wanted it to occur, not as it actually happened'.[68] However, also according to Millon, if a narcissist is challenged for attempting to rewrite history, he may lash out and blame others:

Narcissistic individuals may never have learned to be skilful at public deception; they usually said and did what they liked and without a care for what others thought. Their poorly conceived rationalizations may, therefore, fail to bring relief and, more seriously, may evoke scrutiny and deprecating comments from others. At these times, narcissistic people may be pushed to the point of using projection as a defence ...

So, if denial and distortion fail, the next step for the narcissist is projection. If the team is such that the leader does not have the authority to remove the narcissist – for example, if there is a narcissist on the board of directors but the CEO doesn't have sufficient voting rights to get rid of him – the tendency of the narcissist to project his unacceptable desires onto other team members, including the CEO, will cause major disruption. The ability of the CEO to move the team towards its goals will be severely tested.

Perhaps in such a case, the only solution is for the team (i.e. the board of directors) to force the troublesome board member into a narcissistic breakdown. This is where the narcissist completely loses his self-esteem and feels worthless and helpless, so much so that he is unable to face his colleagues, and leaves. It may be the only solution because, as Kernberg noted, narcissistic patients persistently deny that they have any problems or limitations and consequently lack any motivation for treatment, until faced with a major failure (i.e. a narcissistic breakdown).[69]

However, as lawyer James McDonald Jr pointed out, 'When the narcissist ultimately fails, the fall will be long and hard. Litigation is likely to result, so it is essential that the narcissist's performance problems, disruptive conduct, and abuse of others be thoroughly documented as they occur.'[70]

What Underlies Narcissistic Behaviour?

All narcissists view themselves very highly and expect others to view them the same.

It is relatively easy to describe narcissistic behaviour. We tend to look at the characteristics that we see in an attempt to understand the narcissist, and these are easy to spot once we know what to look for. But these are the symptoms, not the underlying problem.

Narcissistic symptoms display a pervasive pattern of grandiosity, a need for admiration, and a lack of empathy that usually begins by early adulthood. This pattern of grandiosity can be seen in the narcissists' views of their own uniqueness and abilities. Narcissists are beyond being self-centred, viewing themselves very highly and expecting others to view them in the same way. Their preoccupation with themselves and their need for constant attention and admiration from others disturbs their interpersonal relationships, especially given their lack of empathy.[71]

A narcissist displays most, sometimes all, of the following traits:

- An obvious self-focus in interpersonal exchanges
- Problems in sustaining satisfying relationships
- A lack of psychological awareness
- Difficulty with empathy
- Problems distinguishing the self from others
- Hypersensitivity to any slights or imagined insults
- Vulnerability to shame rather than guilt
- Haughty body language
- Flattery towards people who admire and affirm him
- Detesting those who do not admire him
- Using other people without considering the cost to them of him doing so
- Pretending to be more important than he is
- Bragging (subtly but persistently) and exaggerating his achievements
- Claiming to be an 'expert' about most things
- Inability to view the world from the perspective of another person
- Denial of remorse and gratitude

The above narcissistic behaviours are created to display a false image to the world, but these are just the symptoms. Underlying this false image are constant feelings of inferiority, inadequacy and worthlessness. It is because of these feelings that the narcissist develops the false image using the associated behaviours described above, in a never-ending attempt to raise his self-esteem and feel good. The unconscious desire to overcome these underlying inadequate feelings results in paranoia and envy, and these mental conditions characterise the narcissistic condition. Indeed, paranoia and envy underlie all narcissistic behaviours.

The paranoia constantly felt by the narcissist means that he is suspicious of virtually everyone he meets. He fears being caught out and recognised for what he really is (or what he really thinks he is) – that is, the inadequate being who lies beneath the false image. Obsessive mistrust means that he can never accept people for who they are, so there can never being a true and meaningful relationship, even with his family members.

But possibly the most destructive trait common to all narcissists is envy. As a result of feeling inferior, the narcissist can become envious of a spouse, a colleague or a neighbour, particularly a better-educated, more intellectual, better-looking or more successful one. It's not jealousy – you can't be jealous about something you have never had; rather, it is envy; often pathological envy. The following quote from Aristotle exemplifies the difference:

> Jealousy is both reasonable and belongs to reasonable men, while envy is base and belongs to the base, for the one makes himself get good things by jealousy, while the other does not allow his neighbour to have them through envy.[72]

The pathological envy often felt by narcissists is a negative emotional condition brought about by the narcissist's knowledge of the possessions, achievements, or qualities of someone near to him that he does not have. As Kate Barrows said, 'Envy always involves a comparison – we envy that which we lack.'[73]

Envy involves the desire of the narcissist to have for himself something possessed by someone else. If he can't have it, he will try to destroy the possession, achievement, or quality in question, either literally or figuratively. For example, a highly narcissistic husband will fervently object to his wife starting upon a higher education course if the likely outcome is that she will become more qualified than him; or a highly narcissistic householder will object vehemently to an application for planning permission by his neighbour if the result is to be that the neighbour's house will look better than his.

Robert Frank carried out research into people's attitudes towards their neighbours. When asked whether they'd rather have a 4,000-square-foot house in a neighbourhood consisting of 6,000-square-foot mansions, or a 3,000-square-foot home in a zone of 2,000-square-foot bungalows, most people chose the latter; presumably they felt it was more important to feel superior to their neighbours.[74]

A more figurative example of envy may be when the narcissist envies a spouse's university degree, when he doesn't have one of his own. This may show itself by him describing to his wife someone whom he met at a recent party, and who has a university degree, as being unintelligent and having no common sense, as this infers that his spouse is not as intelligent as him, the narcissist, either, nor does she have the common sense that he has.

But what causes this paranoia and envy in narcissists? There are those influences we have already looked at earlier in the section on causes of narcissism, and there may be other reasons, such as genes or the influence of the media, but unhealthy parenting is probably at the root of most narcissistic behaviour today.

3

Codependency

Are You Codependent?

'Codependents often don't know where they end and others begin. There is a lack of clearly defined ego boundaries.' [1]

Codependents are individuals who become dependent upon narcissists, alcoholics or drug addicts. The concept of codependency is derived from the 'co-alcoholic' behaviour of spouses and children in chemically dependent family systems.[2] Counsellors observed that family members often took on the psychological defences and survival behaviours of the alcoholic, thereby extending the malady from the individual to the entire family.

In the same way, codependents take on the psychological defences and survival behaviours of the narcissist, thereby extending the narcissism from the individual to the entire household or workplace.

The following definition of codependency describes how codependents feel and what they feel they must try to achieve:

A pattern of painful dependence on compulsive behaviours and on approval from others in an attempt to find safety, self-worth, and identity.[3]

The following definition of codependency goes some way to explaining what causes it:

> A pattern of coping which develops because of prolonged exposure to and practice of dysfunctional family rules that make difficult the open expression of thought.[4]

Codependency is a condition that affects a large percentage of the adult population in varying degrees. Other terms often used for codependent behaviour in relation to narcissism are: 'enabler', 'follower', 'covert narcissist', 'inverted narcissist', and 'co-narcissist'.[5]

Codependents seek security both at work and at home, so they are drawn to individuals who are, or appear to be, confident, positive and self-assured. Narcissists exhibit these very qualities, displaying an air of superiority, grandiosity and self-importance. Codependents admire these qualities, and narcissists crave admiration.

Narcissists don't want their superiority challenged, so they engage in relationships with individuals who are prepared to remain subservient to them. Codependents, who have been brought up in an environment that ensures they will avoid confrontation if at all possible, are therefore ideal partners. Codependents also find it difficult to make decisions, always checking with others before making choices. The narcissist's constant need for attention fits ideally with this characteristic of the codependent, who ends up checking with the narcissist before making decisions.

However, by subordinating her (or his) needs to those of the narcissist, the codependent puts herself into a position whereby she feels the need to defend the behaviour of her narcissistic spouse, partner, boss or colleague. She therefore feels compelled to take on the psychological defences and survival behaviours of the narcissist. This ultimately results in codependent behaviour characterised by dishonesty and denial.

Melody Beattie wrote a book based on her own experiences as a codependent and the experiences of others in a similar situation. She identified a deep-rooted need to be rescued and to look after others to regulate the codependent's self-esteem. She also describes the overpowering feelings of guilt and anger that codependents torture themselves with.

She believes that this behaviour is habitual and self-destructive, and that it can 'lead us into, or keep us in, destructive relations, relationships that don't work. These behaviours sabotage relationships that may otherwise have worked.' She also explains that codependents unconsciously pick troubled partners in order to have purpose, be needed and feel fulfilled.[6]

Steven was a senior manager who was codependent. He chose to share an office with Wayne, who exhibited strong narcissistic tendencies. Wayne disliked one of the company's managers, George, intensely, and took every opportunity to malign him.

George was responsible for a contract over the weekend that involved working day and night until Monday morning. He was a staff employee, and did not get paid for working nightshifts. However, he agreed to work from midnight on the Sunday until the finish of the job in order to release Chris, who was required to work the Monday nightshift at another site. The job should have finished at 6 o'clock on the Monday morning but ran over into the afternoon. The client insisted it had to be finished, so George stayed with it and worked a very long shift. There was then a dispute between George and Chris's manager about what they had said to each other regarding the return of an essential piece of equipment, which was needed for Chris's Monday nightshift.

On the Tuesday morning, Steven, having discussed the situation with his narcissistic office mate Wayne, described what had happened. He said that George had lied, and that the other manager had told the truth. However, both men insisted that they were telling the truth. Nevertheless, Steven said that he agreed with Wayne, that George should get a written warning. Referring to George, Steven said, '. . . he's not a team worker'.

It is unlikely that this situation would have got to this stage of accusation and recrimination without the intervention of the highly narcissistic Wayne. His willingness to cast blame upon the person he disliked the most was probably at the root of the trouble. But Steven, with no evidence to support his contention other than his exposure to the biased view of his highly narcissistic colleague, concluded that George was at fault, that he should be given a written warning, and that he was not a team worker.

But if he took one step back and analysed what he knew had happened instead of following Wayne's view blindly, Steven's analysis might look rather different. George had worked all Sunday night and all day Monday when he did not have to, and he didn't get paid for it either. He did it to enable Chris to work the Monday nightshift for the other manager, with whom he had the dispute. To most reasonable observers, that *is* a team worker. And anyone who wanted to give him a written warning for putting himself out for the company would, to most people, be the antithesis of a team worker. Steven, the codependent, appears to have been doing the bidding of Wayne, the narcissist. In this case he was doing what codependents do so well – extending the narcissism from an individual to the entire workplace.

Does a Narcissist Control Your Behaviour at Work?

The codependent functions to protect the narcissist from the consequences of his or her behaviour.

The term 'codependency' is used increasingly to describe various dysfunctional relationships.[7] Dysfunctional managerial behaviour is often characterised by narcissistic leaders and their codependents, and is now widespread in the workplace. As a result, codependent employees spread their narcissistic boss's damaging behaviour throughout the workplace. The narcissistic boss needs codependent individuals around him as a source of admiration, and the codependent is attracted to the security he offers – the 'you look after me and I'll look after you' behavioural approach.

As we know, codependents crave security, so they have a tendency to be drawn to the strong and powerful image presented by the narcissistic boss. Unfortunately for the codependent, the image is false. The narcissist uses the codependent's natural desire to help others for his own ends, usually as a boost to his self-esteem.

Codependents live for others, feeling responsible for them and attempting to regulate the world around them.[8] When the codependent is working for (or working with) a narcissist, he is in a position where he can easily be exploited, as a characteristic of the narcissist is lack of empathy.

Codependent characteristics vary from individual to individual, but all of these dysfunctional behaviours have negative consequences and outcomes in the workplace. Codependent patterns of behaviour include avoiding decision making and confrontation, external referencing (always checking outside oneself before making choices), subordinating one's needs to those of the person (the narcissist) with whom one is involved, perfectionism, over-control, manipulation, lack of trust and lying.[9]

> Helping managers who come from dysfunctional backgrounds ... presents a new and different problem for organisations. There is no management development model for dealing with dysfunctional managers. They cannot be 'cured' through projects or seminars. Dysfunctional patterns result from early [childhood] patterns, not lack of skills, knowledge, or ability.[10]

Both narcissists and codependents bring their own dysfunctional childhood patterns into the workplace. The codependent's behaviour can be damaging to the organisation when influenced by, for example, a narcissistic boss. On the other hand, the codependent can be a considerable asset to the organisation when influenced by, for example, a good, effective leader. The earlier description of Steven doing his narcissistic colleague's bidding is an example of how a narcissist can control someone's behaviour at work.

Are Codependents Good Team Workers?

> *Virtually all the commentators writing about codependency agree that people who are codependent trust no one.*[11]

Codependents feel a compelling need to defend the behaviour of a narcissistic spouse, colleague or boss, so they take on the psychological defences and survival behaviours of the narcissist. This ultimately results in codependent behaviour characterised by dishonesty and denial. Thus the behaviour of codependents in teams mimics in many ways the behaviour of the narcissist.

The glue that holds all the pieces in place for an effective and efficient team is trust. All the other characteristics of successful team members are reliant upon their ability to trust both themselves and one another, something virtually all the commentators agree upon.

Possibly the most significant difference between the behaviour of codependents and the behaviour of narcissists is in decision making. Codependents don't trust themselves to make a decision. On the other hand, narcissists are decisive when making decisions: they know what they want; it's whatever is best for them. But codependents use external referencing whenever possible – that is, they always check with others before making choices.[12]

Research by Cook and Goff into the characteristics of successful team members versus codependents identified a number of problems created by codependent individuals in a team-working environment.[13] When they looked at open-mindedness, they found that codependents tend to operate in a dualistic world where everything is seen as either black or white. With regard to emotional stability, they described codependents as 'individuals with constant anxiety and boundary issues, constantly inhibited in relationships by lack of self-esteem and fear of rejection'.

Other problems caused by codependents related to accountability, where they believed that they 'have not learned the distinction between accountability and blame, and because of their insecurities always try to shift responsibility to others'. Their problem-solving abilities were also considered to be suspect, as they were described as 'unable to make decisions and implement actions to carry them out'. And where successful team members had good communication skills, they found that codependents tended 'to hoard information, seeing it as a valuable commodity in short supply'.[14]

They also described successful team members as being good at conflict resolution, whereas codependents were 'caught in a web of self-defeating behaviours', and they noted that codependents learn very early in life that it is dangerous to trust anyone, and carry that into adulthood.[15]

Codependents often experience a sense of being lost, having low self-esteem and being unable to form healthy and productive relationships.[16] One of the most difficult problems they experience is 'boundary distortion' – they are unable to discern where their own person stops and others begin.[17]

They rarely allow others to glimpse their true feelings, displaying rather what they believe others expect of them. Through this 'false self', they internalise the disappointment and anger, holding it like a time bomb for later use. When it finally explodes, it has the capacity to sabotage the whole team process.[18]

However, a book by Dr Stan Katz and Aimee Liu[19] seeks to dispel what they call 'the popular belief' that codependency is a progressive disease. They assert that many codependents are normal people who simply need guidance during difficult periods when they feel out of control. The feeling of being out of control is one that is associated with being too close to, and for too long in the company of, a narcissist.

4

Leadership

Authoritarian and Democratic Leadership

A leader can be authoritarian or democratic, but a narcissist only knows how to be authoritarian.

Leadership and narcissism are inextricably linked because narcissists always feel that they must lead, whether it is the family group, a social group, a work team, a business, a charity organisation, in fact, any situation where a group of people come together with a goal.

The roots of the narcissist's compelling desire to be the leader lie in his core feelings of failure and worthlessness; he compensates for this underlying negative emotional state by projecting a false image of superiority onto those around him. In this way he can feel as though he is in control, and if all goes well, he will be in control of others, although not necessarily completely in control of himself.

As we already know, the protection of this superior image is essential to his survival; accordingly, a superior being feels he must lead those who are lesser beings than he is. As the narcissist sees it, it would be illogical for an inferior being to be in charge of a superior being, so he feels compelled to push himself forward to lead the team or group.

On the face of it, individuals with narcissistic personalities make good leaders. They display the characteristics that most people associate with leadership – for example, an outward confidence when dealing with people, and apparent pleasure in standing up to others. But behind the façade of a confident leader who cares about his family or team lies a selfish authoritarian despot who only cares about himself.

Putting himself at the centre to procure admiration is the narcissist's primary goal, which he will achieve at the expense of anyone whom he perceives as a threat to achieving it. He'll look every bit the leader to whom everyone can turn; he'll say all of the things that those he leads want to hear; and he'll give freely to those who admire him. To those codependents who look to him for their security he will be generous with everything that is under his control, even if he hasn't the authority to give it away. Giving to others has the effect of making them admire his (apparent) kindness and generosity, and at the same time makes them beholden to him. It increases his ability to influence their behaviour when he needs their support.

Leaders fall into two broad categories: authoritarian (or autocratic)[1] leaders, and democratic (or participative) leaders. The democratic category also includes the laissez-faire leaders. Essential requirements for successful, effective leaders are that they are cleverer than average, but not too clever, and that they are more enterprising and creative than average. Once these two criteria are met, the personality of the leader will determine how effective he or she is, depending upon whether they are task orientated or driven by emotion.

Leaders fall into four subdivisions. First, there are the leaders who are authoritarian and whose decision making is task orientated. They are effective and should achieve success, at least in the short term, but they may leave longer-term problems as their authoritarian behaviour tends to result in 'selfish' decision making caused by not listening enough to others. They are the ideal short-term solution in rapidly changing or conflict situations where decisions need to be made quickly and followed through. Examples of authoritarian and task-orientated bosses are described in Chapter 2, and include the former CEO at Enron, Jeff Skilling, and the former chief executive at Royal Bank of Scotland, Sir Fred Goodwin.

Second, there are the leaders who are democratic and whose

decision making is task orientated. These leaders are also effective. They are ideal in short-term stable situations, and also in the long term, but they may not work too well in short-term rapidly changing or conflict situations. Sir Richard Branson of the Virgin Group might be an example of such a leader.

Third, there are the leaders who are authoritarian whose decision making is emotional. They tend to be ineffective. They may enjoy some success in the short term if there is sufficient overlap of personal needs with the needs of their team. They will fail in the long term due to all decisions being made to fulfil their own emotional needs.

Finally, there are the leaders who are democratic whose decision making is emotional. They also tend to be ineffective. They may enjoy some success in the short term, depending upon the makeup of the team members. They will fail in the long term due to all their decision making being done on the basis of trying to satisfy the emotional needs of others, including their own team members.

But it's not quite as straightforward as putting a leader into four broad categories. Leaders can fall anywhere on the authoritarian-democratic continuum and anywhere on a task oriented-emotional continuum. In fact, in practice, leaders who are task orientated and fall somewhere towards the centre of the authoritarian-democratic continuum tend to be the most successful leaders in business, and possibly also in other spheres.

Authoritarian or autocratic-style leaders also find that they lose more team members than democratic leaders do. People prefer to work with democratic leaders as they feel that they are being listened to, whereas authoritarian or autocratic-style leaders tend to generate more discontent, hostility and aggression, resulting in team members leaving.[2]

Narcissists can be placed in the third category, as they are authoritarian and are usually ineffective; their decision making is based on their emotional needs. However, narcissists can also be authoritarian and effective in some situations. For example, they are able to temporarily become task orientated when they can see a significant benefit to themselves.

Codependents can be placed in the fourth category, as they are democratic and are usually ineffective; their decision making being based on the emotional needs of others.

Effective Leadership

An effective leader will ensure that the team survives and thrives. An ineffective leader could mean it is unsuccessful, a failure.

Effective leadership is important in any team situation. A husband and wife is a team. A family is a team. A board of directors is a team. To survive and thrive, the team must be effectively led. Ineffective leadership will inevitably result in failure. A husband-and-wife team that fails can have far-reaching implications for their children, and a board of directors that fails can have far-reaching implications for the organisation's employees.

Good team members can only partially compensate for a poor leader. A family team led by a highly narcissistic husband who has a highly intelligent but codependent wife may well survive, and to the outsider may survive well, but it will not thrive due to the emotional turmoil both will endure.

It is said that behind every successful man is a woman. The same may be said of the converse relationship. Margaret Thatcher, for example, was a British Prime Minister who transformed Britain, for better or for worse, depending upon your point of view. Behind her was her husband, a successful businessman in his own right, but without his support she may never have achieved such heights in her political career.

You may have already established whether you have an authoritarian or a democratic leadership style. Few would claim that Margaret Thatcher's leadership style was not authoritarian, and few would claim that she was not effective in achieving her aims. She took on the unions and won, and she fought a war and won, an unprecedented achievement in recent western history. This puts her in the category of leaders who are authoritarian and whose decision making is task orientated; they are effective and should achieve success in the short term. Such leaders are the ideal short-term solution in rapidly changing or conflict situations where decisions need to be made quickly and followed through. Margaret Thatcher was successful, but she was eventually forced out, probably through not listening enough to others or only listening to those who told her what she wanted to hear, a fundamental flaw in the makeup of authoritarian leaders. Such leaders who are successful often go on to believe in their own omnipotence, and their decision making becomes more centred on their emotional self rather than focusing on the task at hand.

You may, on the face of it, categorise yourself as either effective or ineffective as a leader. But we need to look into effectiveness a little more deeply to understand how effective leaders (and ineffective leaders) influence their teams. Some leaders are able to create teams that do more than survive – they thrive, and they become highly successful.

There are various types of team. We have just looked at the teams of which Margaret Thatcher was a member – her family and her political team. Eventually her political team threw her out. There are also sports teams, and teams set up in business. If you are part of a senior management team – for example, a member of the board of directors – or if you are thinking of starting a business, you can learn from what effective leaders have done that made them successful, and from the mistakes of others that have led to their failure. An ineffective leader can be more than just ineffective; an ineffective leader with a personality disorder can mean the death of a team. And as we know, Narcissistic Personality Disorder is very difficult to detect.

The vast majority (over 95 per cent) of businesses that survive in modern economies do not grow beyond the initial stage from start-up to becoming established.[3] This is because the main objective of the leaders of these 'lifestyle' organisations is to create the status they desire and to generate sufficient income to meet their lifestyle needs. Successful organisations which tend to grow year on year are in the minority. These organisations generally have a senior management team of two or more individuals, one of whom (the leader) is 'growth' orientated.

There is very little literature relating to successful high-growth senior management teams due to the difficulty encountered in trying to research them.[4] And whilst there has been a lot written about leaders and executives with personality disorders such as narcissism, there has been little empirical research in this area specific to leaders (CEOs) or senior management team members, such as boards of directors. Michael Maccoby stated about narcissistic leaders that 'psychoanalysts don't usually get close enough to them, especially in the workplace, to write about them'.[5] There appears to be a need, therefore, to disseminate more and better information to managers, and, indeed, more widely to the population as a whole, on how to recognise 'the real disease of many executives ... narcissism'.[6]

It is particularly difficult to identify what is needed to establish a successful team, and how to avoid the pitfalls relating to teaming up with the wrong person or people. Finding the right leader is, of course, of critical importance. The person who puts him or herself forward as the one to lead the team may be completely ineffective as a leader. In fact, that person may be the worst possible leader. Many people think that all leadership involves is giving orders and sounding important, but there is a lot more to being a successful leader. The literature differentiates between the emergent leader (the person who puts him or herself forward for the job) and the effective leader. If you want to be part of a successful team, the only option is to go with the effective leader.[7]

Leadership Style

Having an effective leadership style is of critical importance. An ineffective leadership style will at best limit a team's success, and may lead to its death.

Effective leadership is essentially about leadership style, and is widely recognised as crucial to the success of any team.[8] But even the best leaders are limited in what they can achieve if other team members are not suitable. Each team member, including the leader, will have either a positive or a negative influence on the team's performance. To realise effective leadership, it is necessary to identify the leadership styles and the leadership skills that make a positive contribution, as well as leadership styles and the leadership skills that make a negative contribution.

Good leaders and suitable team members can be identified. It is important to know what to look for in an individual's behaviour and background, and it may be useful to use analytical methods of identification. It will also help to identify those individuals with behavioural or psychological problems, some of whom are fairly easy to identify – for example, neurotics and paranoiacs – and some who can be very difficult to detect, such as narcissists.[9]

The leadership style of neurotic leaders is characterised by anxiousness, worrying, moodiness, and frequent depression, and is linked to obsessive behaviour.[10] Such leaders come in different guises – for example, they may be phobic, obsessive-compulsive, depressive or hypochondriacal. They have fears that they have difficulty coping with, and in an ideal world would get help from a psychotherapist to deal with their problems. Whilst some may feel sorry for them, and even have a desire to help, it is best to avoid them. The fact that they are trying to cope with their own problems will result in them making a negative contribution to the team's performance.

The leadership style of paranoiacs will also have a negative impact on the team. They have all the symptoms of the simple schizophrenic but with more intensity: delusions of grandeur, moodiness, and a strong distrust of other people, even to the point of believing that people are plotting against them. Beware though – paranoiacs often strive excessively for success or leadership, so will be keen to become a member of the team, as leader if at all possible.

The narcissist's leadership style emphasises 'impression management' and also contains a very strong element of paranoia. Narcissists are more concerned with their own image (how they appear to others) than with the results of their work. Thus they tend to have a negative impact on their team or organisation in the long term, and, as we know, they can be extremely difficult to identify.[11] In the short term, as leaders, they exude apparent confidence, knowledge, ability and general all-round management skills, which can be an advantage to the fledgling team trying to get the organisation up and running. But beware: once established in a position of authority, the narcissist will make life extremely difficult for anyone who challenges their 'superiority'.

Narcissistic Personality Disorder (NPD)[12] is an extreme and rigid extension of narcissism. It involves inflated self-esteem, lack of empathy for others, a sense of entitlement to special treatment and privileges, disagreeableness, and, most of all, an all-consuming need for attention. Bear in mind, though, that many normal people have narcissistic traits and that all people behave narcissistically at times and toward certain people.

Narcissists, by their very nature, will attempt to infiltrate the senior echelons of any group or team, and will feel that it is their right to lead them. There are many narcissists and people with other personality disorders who think that they will make a good leader, and it is therefore of critical importance that the team leader who is ultimately installed has the right leadership style and has a vision of success. A narcissistic leader's vision consists solely of him being at the top of the organisation, and he will do whatever is necessary to maintain that position, even to the detriment of the team and the organisation.

A leader with the right qualities and behavioural characteristics is the first step in creating a successful team. A leader with a personality disorder is a recipe for disaster.

Leadership Skill and Enterprise

Leadership skill and a high enterprise tendency are essential attributes of the successful leader.

We have established that the leader must not be neurotic, paranoiac or narcissistic. From the remaining leadership contenders, it is primarily the leader's skill and enterprise that will determine the success or otherwise of the team, be it a business, a family, or a sports team. Leadership skills can be taught, but enterprise, arguably, cannot. Both are of the utmost importance. Research evidence demonstrates it is possible to identify leaders who will ensure that their team will survive (and possibly thrive), and leaders who will almost certainly ensure that their team will ultimately fail.[13]

The first type of leader identified above has a high enterprise tendency, whilst the second type has a low enterprise tendency.

Accordingly, the leader must have good leadership skills and a high enterprise tendency if the team is to survive. A leader with poor leadership skills and who is not enterprising will most likely lead to the death of the team and any organisation that it represents.

Research into the enterprise tendencies of team members in growth organisations has revealed that the main characteristics associated with enterprise are need for achievement, need for autonomy or independence, locus of control, creativity, and moderate or calculated risk taking. 'Locus of control' is a concept introduced in 1966 by Julian Rotter, an American psychologist known for developing influential theories. In this case it relates to internal locus of control, which is the belief that an individual can control or exert influence over his environment, as opposed to an external locus of control where the individual believes that his environment is controlled mainly through external factors outside of his control, for example fate, luck, or other powerful individuals.[14]

Instruments are available commercially that claim to measure enterprise tendency,[15] but none of these addresses all of the main characteristics associated with enterprise. In addition, there is little evidence in the literature regarding the use of these instruments, and hence their validity and reliability is unproven. Other possible instruments from the literature, by King[16] and Freeley,[17] again do not meet all of the criteria for accurate measurement.

However, Sally Caird's 'General Enterprise Tendency' test is one instrument in the literature that relates closely to the main constructs associated with the tendency to be enterprising identified above. In addition, it has considerable support in the literature for its validity and reliability.[18]

But it would be folly to rely solely upon a person's tendency to be entrerprising or not when selecting a leader, as narcissistic individuals also have a tendency to be enterprising. In fact, they need to be enterprising to survive.

5

Teamwork

Why is Teamwork Important?

Belbin demonstrated why teamwork is important; a good manager requires many qualities, but they are often mutually exclusive.

John Donne coined the often-used expression 'no man is an island'.[1] Humans are social beings who need to interact with others. If we try to isolate ourselves from fellow human beings, we find that we are less happy and less successful. We achieve most of our most satisfying goals in life through teamwork.

If we can identify what makes a successful team, we can use this knowledge to benefit ourselves and others in pursuit of achieving our goals in life. But narcissists also rely on teams; they need to become members of teams for their survival, and they are adept at manipulating them for their own ends. If we want to avoid the possibility of narcissistic individuals sabotaging the realisation of our goals when we work in teams, we need to gain an understanding of how they may hijack the process of teamwork for their own personal, selfish ends.

Dr Meredith Belbin demonstrated the importance of teamwork in achieving a successful outcome to a project.[2] He explained why an individual cannot achieve alone what a team can achieve through teamwork. For example, to succeed in achieving the goal of a successful team or small business, two of the qualities an individual must possess are dynamism and patience.[3] It is difficult for one person to be both dynamic and patient, but two people can possess these qualities between them. Thus, teamwork now becomes important.

The literature indicates that most successful businesses are started by teams, rather than by individuals,[4] and that teamwork and team design are important elements in all successful teams.[5] We have already established that strength of leadership is important for the achievement of success in any group or organisation, and thus teamwork should manifest itself through the role played by the leader, as well as by the other team members.

There are two team roles that must be present in a successful organisation's senior management team,[6] though these two team members must be able to work together – that is, they must manifest teamwork. First, we need someone who is enthusiastic, quick off the mark, and an extrovert. He or she must be a good communicator with people both inside and outside the organisation and be adept at exploring new opportunities and developing contacts. Second, we need someone who is practical, with common sense and self-control, and who is hard-working. He or she must tackle problems in a systematic fashion, and also be loyal and more interested in work than in the pursuit of self-interest.

One of these qualities may be present in the leader, but it seems highly unlikely that one person could have characteristics relating to both of these team roles, as they are mutually exclusive. It appears to be the working together of these very different team roles that creates the successful team. As the team roles are so different, a strong and conciliatory leader is essential if the team is to succeed; the leader must recognise the importance of teamwork.

Brian Clough and Peter Taylor were a legendary management team in English football from the late 1960s to the 1980s, winning the League Championship with two different clubs and the European Cup twice. Clough achieved all of his major successes in partnership with Taylor. Between them they had the variety of qualities necessary to succeed, but on their own they were both relative failures as managers.

It appears that the reason organisations run by individuals tend to be less dynamic than those run by teams relates to the limitations on the qualities one individual possesses, as opposed to teams, whose members between them possess a variety of individual qualities.

Belbin noted other qualities that are often mutually exclusive: a leader must be intelligent but must not be too clever. He (or she) must be forceful but must be sensitive to people's feelings. He must be a fluent communicator but a good listener. He must be decisive, but he must be reflective.

Although it is possible to identify individuals with the above positive characteristics using psychometric tests, it is also possible that one or more of the team members carries with them psychological problems – for example, as already mentioned, they may exhibit neurosis, paranoia and/or narcissism, all of which could have an adverse effect on the team. Narcissism in the workplace is an increasingly common problem, and it impacts badly on all teamwork. These problems need to be identified at an early stage as the narcissist, as we already know, is the exact opposite of a good team worker.

Projection in Teams

Projection can be achieved by provoking another team member into being critical, and then sitting back, reassured that you are not the one who constantly criticises others.

Projection is one of the defence mechanisms that enable us to survive the constant emotional challenges of life. Others are denial, distortion, splitting, regression, and so on. Projection is not normally a problem – everyone uses it from time to time – but it can become so entrenched in the behaviour of some individuals – for example, narcissists – that it limits their personality development.

Generally, projection operates in the unconscious, which can be manifest at both the individual level and in groups within teams.

61

There are many different ways in which projective processes manifest themselves in teams. For example, a team member may constantly criticise others, but by provoking another team member into being critical, he can keep the shame he feels about his behaviour hidden from other team members and from himself. He projects his own unacceptable behaviour onto someone else.

Projection is a way of dealing with thoughts and behaviour that we wish to deny or distance ourselves from. It involves an attempt to control and manipulate others that is caused by a fear of being controlled, albeit an unconscious fear. It is done to deny or distance the individual from his true feelings.

Projection is often used in conjunction with splitting, a Freudian defence mechanism in which an object or idea (or, alternatively, the ego) is separated into two or more parts in order to remove its threatening meaning.[7]

Dr Roy Lubit identified splitting as a defence mechanism present in all narcissists, stating: 'The defense mechanism that dominates the functioning of [narcissistic] individuals is splitting. They see people and situations in black and white terms, all bad or all good, with no shades of gray.'[8]

Narcissistic individuals see fellow team members as either good (for example, as codependent) or bad (that is, as a threat to their vulnerable feelings of inadequacy and worthlessness). Note that this doesn't mean that the narcissistic individual is inadequate and worthless; it is simply that he *feels* that way. This good/bad or black/white image of others leads such individuals either to idealise or to fear and hate their fellow team members. But they are quite capable of idealising someone one day and hating them the next. They can easily be thrown into pain and anxiety when they feel threatened by criticism or rejection; memories of failure or shame spark unresolved core issues, exacerbating this painful emotional experience.

Thus, narcissists constantly use splitting and projection in team situations – primarily because of their need to control the other team members; they can't run the risk of feeling the pain and anxiety associated with criticism or rejection.

It is important that the team leader understands how projection works in teams. Projection is used by everyone from time to time and is not normally a significant problem; it's a natural defence mechanism for normal, psychologically healthy people. But narcissists tend to use projection in team situations so extensively that they prevent meaningful discussion, and the effectiveness of the team is diminished.

The Narcissist's Influence on Team Members

'Memory is a reconstructive process that uses every piece of information at its disposal to build the mental images.'[9]

The way that narcissists influence other team members is difficult to detect for most people, but if we are armed with knowledge of how the human being's memory works, understanding the narcissist becomes surprisingly straightforward.

Our memories of past experiences are part fact and part illusion. Our brain can remember a huge amount of information, but it can't record everything we experience. It gets around this problem by storing just enough information to recall an experience that happened in the past, and then it fills in the gaps with imagination.[10] So if, after using every piece of information at our disposal we still make up a large part of what we think we remember, there is plenty of scope for the narcissist to influence what the imagination uses to fill these gaps.

The narcissist's brain is on constant alert for opportunities for self-aggrandisement or the denigration of others.[11] He (or she) is also on the lookout for opportunities to support his codependents to maintain his power base. All opportunities that are presented in the course of discussion are taken in order to further the narcissist's ability to influence, or perhaps more accurately, manipulate the memory recall of his codependents and others. The following research study describes how words can influence memory recall:

People were shown a film of a traffic accident. They were then asked questions about it. Among the questions there was one about the speed of the cars, and this was phrased very carefully. Half of the people were asked, 'How fast were the cars going when they hit one another?' while the other half were asked, 'How fast were the cars going when they smashed into one another?' All the other questions were the same.

A week later, the same people were asked to remember the film they had seen. Among other things, they were asked whether there had been any broken glass in the film. There hadn't been any, and those who had been asked about the cars hitting one another remembered that. But those who had been asked about the cars smashing into one another distinctly remembered broken glass strewn around the road, and were surprised to find that it wasn't there when they saw the film again. The words which were used when they were asked about the accident had directly influenced what they remembered – to the point of introducing details which hadn't been there originally.[12]

Narcissists also introduce details that hadn't been there originally. These details directly influence what others remember, skewed positively in favour of the narcissist and negatively against his 'enemies'. For example, a narcissist called Marcus described the damage to his car after an accident that was his fault, saying, 'Ah, it's nothing.' The car required a new driver's-side door, a new front wing, a new headlight, other body repairs and a paint respray. However, a week earlier the narcissist's colleague, Victor, had an accident that was not his fault. The narcissist disliked Victor, and when describing the damage, said, 'What a f***ing mess.' Repairing the damage to Victor's car, involving the replacement of a damaged plastic fuel pipe underneath the car, took 25 minutes at the garage. The cost of repairs to Marcus's car was more than 20 times the cost of the repair to Victor's car.

The narcissist uses emotive language to directly influence what the other team members remember about the narcissist himself and other individuals, using positive prompts for himself and his supporters and negative prompts for his enemies. Narcissists 'remember the past as they would have wanted it to occur, not as it actually happened'.[13] Over time, this technique used by the narcissist will influence in varying degrees all team members, by which means his distorted world view will gain acceptance. Codependents are particularly susceptible to this technique. Narcissists have the capacity to manipulate not only team members, but also one-to-one encounters, and when the opportunity presents itself, they can influence the thoughts and behaviour of large numbers of people. There are many precedents in history to demonstrate that the way people think and behave can be manipulated. Adolf Hitler, for example, was able to influence the thinking and behaviour of a large part of the population of Germany, an advanced society. Like Adolf Hitler, narcissists use the power of words to emotionally colour individuals', team members', and whole populations' perceptions of themselves for the better, and those of their enemies – Jews, for example, in the case of Hitler – for the worse.

Contemporary methods used to change people's thinking for the better include neuro-linguistic programming (NLP) and cognitive behavioural therapy (CBT). NLP is based on the idea that mind, body and language interact to create an individual's perception of the world and that those perceptions, and hence behaviours, can be changed. It uses methods and models to bring about positive change in individuals. CBT seeks to identify and change 'distorted' or 'unrealistic' ways of thinking by talking through situations and influencing thoughts, emotions, physical feelings and actions (in that order), thereby influencing behaviour for the better.

But if thinking and perception can be changed for the better, the reverse can also apply. Narcissists' distort the perceptions of the people around them. Harvard professor Daniel Gilbert tells us that 'memory is a reconstructive process that uses every piece of information at its disposal to build the mental images that come ... to mind when we engage in the act of remembering'.[14] So if distorted information is continually fed into that 'reconstructive process' by a narcissist, the mental images will be reconstructed, and in time will reflect the narcissist's view.

The narcissist is aware more than anyone that the same behavioural traits can be described in different ways. For example, someone not conforming to the norms expected by those around him can be described generously as 'naughty', or in an unkind way as 'bad'. There are many examples of descriptions of behavioural traits of individuals described by narcissists that depend upon whether the individual is perceived as a friend or an enemy. A friend may be described as cheeky, whereas an enemy (real or perceived) may be arrogant; a friend is firm, an enemy is pigheaded; a friend is slim, an enemy is scrawny; a friend is well-built, an enemy is fat; a friend is a perfectionist, an enemy is a control freak.

In each of the above alternatives, the literal meaning of the word used to describe a friend is the same as that used to describe an enemy, but the emotional meaning is attractive towards friends and offensive against enemies.

A narcissist can distort the perceptions of the people around him over time using the above relatively subtle technique. However, if he believes that what he says will not get back to his 'enemy', perhaps when he is in the company of a codependent 'friend', he will use less subtle techniques, often involving the use of expletives for greater effect. For example, instead of saying 'He's arrogant', he may use stronger and more emotionally colourful language to have more impact on his team member's perception of the individual, by saying, 'He's a lazy arrogant son of a bitch.'

The individual may not be lazy or arrogant at all, but merely the object of the narcissist's envy. Narcissists' tend to subscribe to the view of Gustave Flaubert, who said, 'There is no truth. There is only perception.'

6

A Narcissistic Team Member

Is She a Narcissist?

The deteriorating performance of the organisation appears to result from one senior manager's narcissistic behaviour.

Scargill, Spears and Jones[1] is an architectural consultancy organisation that has been suffering a rapid decline in profitability, resulting in increasing losses over the last two years. Victoria is a new employee of the company who has been tasked with investigating the reasons why the business is underperforming and with making recommendations for improving the organisation's performance.

Although the business is well established and has been profitable for many years, its trading performance has been deteriorating in recent years and it has just made a loss for the second year running; this loss is significantly greater than the previous year's loss. The senior partner has given Victoria this task without any preconditions. But Victoria has to remember that her report will be read by the three partners in the practice, so she must be tactful in any reference to their shortcomings.

Tom Scargill is the senior partner in the firm and recently celebrated his 60th birthday. His experience is broad and he has an interest in, and understanding of, both new build and refurbishment work, including conservation. He has a reputation for being fair and a good listener, but also for being indecisive, although he did successfully dismiss an incompetent employee about three years ago.

He works hard on his own projects but tends to leave the management of the practice to Nadia, one of the other partners.

Andy Spears is the middle partner in terms of seniority, and is 50 years old. He is officially responsible for human resources, but in practice the decisions are made by Nadia. He is said to be kind and considerate but ineffectual, usually deferring to Tom and unwilling or unable to tackle Nadia successfully on his own.

Nadia Jones, at 48 years old, is the junior of the three partners, but she plays a major executive role in managing the firm. She has been described as a 'control freak' by one of the salaried employees, and another one said, 'What s the difference between Nadia and a terrorist? You can negotiate with a terrorist!' The employees also say that Nadia does not listen, does not respect their knowledge and experience, and does not understand conservation work.

Georgina joined the practice about a year ago at the age of 31. She does most of the conservation work, works long hours and is something of a perfectionist. She believes that Nadia does not negotiate high enough fees for the conservation projects, which include several well-known Grade 1 listed buildings and scheduled ancient monuments.

Jasmine joined the practice three years ago and works mainly on the more high-profile new-build projects. She believes herself to be talented and creative, and therefore does not see why she should have to work very hard. She frequently does not arrive at the office until noon and does not leave particularly late or take a lot of work home. Tom does not seem to recognise her shortcomings, but tends to parade her in front of clients as the firm's token ethnic minority. Other employees clearly resent the fact that her laziness appears to be overlooked by the partners. The partnership also employs three secretarial staff and a junior technician.

The partnership does not use timesheets. Individual project profitability and individual fee-earner profitability are calculated on the basis of estimated apportionment of individuals' time to projects. The estimation is done by Nadia, who always appears to be the most profitable fee-earner. The firm has had a high turnover of staff for several years.

The clients for the conservation projects all praise Georgina, but most of these projects make a loss, according to Nadia's analysis. Jasmine's projects generally break even but are rarely completed on time. Contractors, consultant quantity surveyors and consultant engineers frequently complain that Jasmine is lacking in technical competence and is not interested in producing clear, practical and comprehensive working drawings to a sensible programme.

Tom appears to be representative of Dr Meredith Belbin's 'Team Worker' and 'Implementer' team roles and lacks the characteristics identified with the leadership team roles of 'Shaper' and 'Coordinator'.[2] As a team worker, he is supportive, sociable and concerned about others, a good listener, but indecisive. As an implementer, he has practical common sense, self-control and discipline, is hard working, tackles problems in a systematic fashion, but lacks spontaneity and shows signs of rigidity.

Andy is kind and considerate but ineffectual, leaving decision making to Nadia. Again, no leadership characteristics are evident.

Nadia appears to take on the leadership role, displaying the characteristics of Belbin's Shaper[3] team role. She appears to be competitive, determined, argumentative, but lacking in interpersonal sensitivity. Shapers may develop narcissistic tendencies if they are allowed to work without any form of control, as seems to be the case here; Tom and Andy appear to exert little in the way of controls over her actions.

If the above analysis of Nadia is accurate, her pattern of behaviour may be typical of someone with acute narcissistic tendencies. She may therefore display the behavioural characteristic of 'splitting', which has been described in the literature as the defence mechanism that dominates the functioning of narcissistic individuals (see chapter 2, n.43). Freud referred to splitting as a mental process by which two separate and contradictory versions of reality could co-exist. This conceptualisation of splitting defines an ego that allows reality to be both acknowledged and denied.

It appears that the fundamental problems faced by the consultancy relate to a lack of effective financial controls and a lack of effective leadership. Victoria's description of the situation at the practice suggests that Nadia is envious of Georgina. Georgina works long hours and is something of a perfectionist, and clients praise her, but according to Nadia, most of her projects make a loss. If this is the case, it is possible that Nadia is attempting to 'deny the object' – the object being Georgina. (Note that 'object' is used here in its broadest sense, which is simply to indicate the 'other' to whom the self is related. In the English language object tends to be depersonalised; an object is a thing. However, when Klein, a psychologist, used the word 'object', it was as derived from the German 'objekt'. For example, in its grammatical usage, a verb relates a subject to an object, whether the object in question is a person or a thing.) Victoria's analysis implies that Nadia uses her position to distort the calculations relating to Georgina's work, thus denying her the recognition she deserves (i.e. denying the object). If this is the case, it is quite typical of a narcissist.

Although Nadia's team role appears to be as a shaper, thus showing strong leadership qualities, in this case the potential benefits of her leadership characteristics may be lost through her narcissistic tendencies. It is a characteristic of narcissism that at the same time as narcissistic personality traits may help managers to rise within an organisation, these same traits may impair their ability to lead effectively, and as Belbin stated in his book *Management Teams: Why They Succeed or Fail*, the only option is the effective leader.

Victoria needs to recommend measures to improve business performance in the future. As she recognises, she will need to be tactful. If she decides to challenge Nadia she will have to be very sure of her ground, with solid evidence to support her. It is well documented that narcissists resort to denial and distortion of facts, and can be extremely persuasive, so as a newly employed member of staff and a relative outsider, Victoria will need to be very careful indeed.

Nadia does, however, appear to be the problem; her narcissistic behaviour is undermining the good work done by Georgina, but she appears to be unconcerned about Jasmine's improper behaviour. As Nadia is a partner with the power to dismiss Victoria, it would be wise for Victoria not to point out directly in her report where the problem lies. If there was greater input from the more senior partners, the problems reported by Victoria could be reduced. To achieve this it would be necessary to improve communications within the business.

As a first step, accurate recording of time spent on projects would facilitate better financial analysis of project costs (although Nadia may take such a recommendation as a personal slight against her). Following on from this, the production of management accounts at the end of each month would enable loss-making projects to be identified at an early stage.

The overriding issue is that of leadership, and this needs to be addressed, but as Nadia is a partner, the options appear to be limited. Perhaps the best Victoria could achieve would be to raise the awareness of the two senior partners such that they take a more active role in the management of the practice and thereby reduce the domination and control that Nadia seems to have. If the partners don't already have regular minuted meetings, it may be worthwhile for Victoria to recommend that a meeting is held each month as soon as the management accounts are produced in order to discuss them.

Victoria has been able, in this case, to identify the symptoms of a malignant narcissist at work – Nadia. But malignant narcissists are masters of manipulation, deception and control in the workplace, particularly when they have manoeuvred themselves into a position of seniority where their authoritarian leadership characteristics can be used to control their environment. Nadia appears to have exhibited typical narcissistic symptoms by getting control of the means by which individuals in the organisation are judged and by manipulating information to defame those whom she dislikes in the eyes of those she needs to impress in order to remain in control.

The malignant narcissist's symptoms are easy enough to see when they are analysed in the context of the narcissist's environment. In this case, Nadia's mask, the false image she presents to her colleagues, appears to have been seen through by several colleagues, including Victoria, as well as the salaried employees who described her as a control freak and compared her to a terrorist.

Nadia appears to be denying Georgina the recognition that she deserves by undervaluing her work, yet she fails to recognise the lack of commitment by Jasmine. As Jasmine's laziness appears to be overlooked by Tom, the senior partner, it may be that Nadia chooses to ignore her laziness.

It may be that Nadia denies Georgina the recognition she deserves as she sees her as a close competitor. Nadia fears that if Georgina is recognised by the two senior partners for what she is – a very competent and hard-working employee – she will receive the admiration that Nadia wants to keep for herself. Jasmine, being lazy, does not appear to pose a threat to Nadia.

To fully understand why Nadia discriminates against the hard-working and popular Georgina, yet ignores the lazy Jasmine, it would be necessary to know much more about her upbringing – her childhood, her education, her parenting, her adolescence. Armed with this information, it would then be possible to recognise how her history informs her thinking, and thus to understand why she chooses to deny recognition to those who deserve it. The more successful and popular the narcissist's victim is, the more the narcissist denies, denigrates, belittles and maligns her.

The reasons for the narcissist's malevolent and malicious behaviour always lie in the narcissist's background, which usually remains hidden; it will most certainly not be divulged by the narcissist him or herself.

7

Narcissism at Work

Understanding the Real Meaning behind the Words

The narcissist's speech is littered with the pronouns 'I', 'he' and 'she'; 'I' for self-aggrandisement and 'he' or 'she' for denigrating others.

In order to fully understand how a narcissist's background impacts on his behaviour it is necessary to look in detail at the words he uses. As Susie Orbach, an eminent psychoanalyst, said, 'You have to listen carefully. Listen to what is being said, to words used, to the pauses, the hesitations, the omissions, the tone, the feel and the wishes buried within the sentences.'[1] The personality of an individual is encoded in his language; by listening to what he says we can build a complete picture of his personality traits. You don't have to be a therapist; you only need some background knowledge of the narcissist, and then to make a note of some of the emotive phrases and sentences he uses.

Further evidence of the ability to accurately predict behaviour through observing just a few short interactions is provided by Dr John Gottman and his fellow researchers. They examined facial expressions, dialogue and physical reactions of couples in conversation. They found that it was possible to predict the outcome of a relationship with amazing accuracy – between 88 and 94 per cent – from just a few short interactions.[2]

There is no disputing the narcissist's verbal dexterity and skill when applying his well-honed skills of self-aggrandisement and

73

denigration of others. His brilliance is found in his ability to make it appear through his words as though he is not indulging in self-aggrandisement while at the same time he is denigrating his prey using subtle lies and distortion. As his prey is always a close competitor, someone who is receiving the attention and admiration that he craves, by successfully denigrating him he achieves his other goal by implication – namely, that of self-aggrandisement.

The difficulty encountered by any onlooker is in trying to identify who the victim is. The victim – that is, the person denigrated by the narcissist or his codependent – will logically fight back using truth as his justification. But the narcissist's denigration always incorporates an element of truth; he just distorts it and perhaps adds a lie or two.

The problem for the victim is that it is he who is the successful one – if he wasn't successful the narcissist wouldn't envy him and so wouldn't take the trouble to deny him due recognition and malign him. So when the victim tells the truth – to a mutual colleague, for example – it appears that he is boasting about his successes, his qualities or possessions, that he is being grandiose and applying the same self-aggrandisement used by the narcissist. This is particularly so if the narcissist has prepared the ground – and he usually has – by subtly suggesting to the mutual colleague that his victim is envious of him. To this colleague or onlooker, it now appears that the person being victimised by the narcissist is actually the perpetrator, and that the narcissist is the victim.

The narcissist has the capacity to make his victim appear to be envious of him, when in fact it is the other way round. But if we know enough about his background, by analysing the words he uses we can understand what is going on, who the perpetrator is and who the victim is. By selecting just a few emotive phrases or sentences from what the narcissist says about his victim, we can gain an in-depth understanding of his perverse logic and his motives.

Nathan

'In Kets de Vries and Miller's analysis of different types of narcissistic leader, a category of individuals is identified who "live under the illusion that they are entitled to be served" and who care "little about hurting and exploiting others in the pursuit of [their] own advancement".'[3]

Harvey was a CEO who spent a number of years building up a successful business with his co-director Nathan, who was a malignant narcissist, and two other directors, Cody and Todd. Nathan undermined Harvey and denigrated him to chosen others at every opportunity. Note that Nathan only denigrated Harvey to chosen others; his political mastery meant that he recognised the danger of universal denigration, as this would make him appear to be the envious one. His objective was to make Harvey appear to be envious of him, thus maintaining his grandiose self-image.

It appeared to Harvey that Nathan was waiting for his big chance, that would come when the company fell on hard times and he could deliver the final telling blow to enable him to take Harvey's place as CEO. Unfortunately for Nathan, this never happened during Harvey's tenure as CEO. The company continued to thrive through developing a branch network and becoming ever more successful, notwithstanding Nathan's best efforts to undermine Harvey's endeavour.

Taking unfounded credit for many of the company's successes wasn't enough for Nathan. For example, in order to impress Todd, who, unlike the other three directors, was based at a branch away from the head office, Nathan told him that he had established and developed another successful branch of the company, when in fact he had not. Again, we should note his selectiveness in this case. He only set out to impress one person, Todd, who he knew was not aware of the true circumstances. Nathan made no attempt to impress others with the same lie. But despite Harvey finding out about Nathan's lie and communicating the facts to the other board members, the ever-resourceful narcissist never gave up. His dysfunctionality would not let him do so, because he could never allow the false image he projected to be compromised. If it were compromised, the result would almost certainly mean that he would feel anxiety, stress, even despair if he wasn't able to re-establish the belief in the false image by those who provided his narcissistic feedback. Nathan tried lies, distortion and projection to undermine Harvey, but met with only limited success, so he turned to character assassination.[4]

Over the years of frustration that Nathan appeared to experience waiting for the company's growth to falter, he developed Cody, one of the other directors, as his trusted sidekick. Cody exhibited codependent characteristics and shared an office with Nathan. He admired Nathan, and over time, by exerting his malevolent influence on him, Nathan was able to convince Cody of the veracity of his distorted world view. This put him in a stronger position in his quest to undermine Harvey.

With Cody on board, Nathan turned to the remaining director, Todd. Whilst Nathan was confident that he had succeeded in distorting the views of Cody, he still had to win over Todd. He arranged a meeting between himself, Cody and Todd, ostensibly about internal and relatively insignificant company matters, which he knew Harvey would not attend. The meeting was at the head office, but prior to it, Nathan had prepared the ground with a series of visits to the branch where Todd presided. This was unusual, as Nathan had shown little interest in the branch's development up to that point.

At the meeting, with the full support of Cody, his codependent office companion, Nathan took the opportunity to indulge in the assassination of Harvey's character. None of the statements made to Todd about Harvey by Nathan or Cody on their own were of huge significance, but the barrage of criticisms, and the sheer ruthlessness and quantity of derogatory assertions about him, although untrue, achieved the desired outcome of assassinating Harvey's character in the eyes of Todd, who was oblivious to what was really going on. The implication, although never stated, was that Nathan was the intellect and driving force behind the success of the company. Although Todd had no cause to do so before the meeting, at the end it left him questioning Harvey's competence as CEO. Although each of the many denigrating statements had been fairly innocuous in themselves, when combined, they had the desired effect of assassinating the character of an innocent person.

The construction of each denigrating statement always followed the same pattern, of usually being a lie, with some further distortion of the truth about an event that actually happened, combined with projection. Such statements always related to an event where the narcissist, Nathan, felt inferior to his victim, Harvey. Nathan then used projection to make himself feel superior.

Nathan's intention was to assassinate Harvey's character behind his back. Harvey was not supposed to know what went on at the meeting, as minutes were not taken. But when he did become aware of what had been said at the meeting, it put him in the difficult situation of deciding how to deal with the behaviour of both Nathan and Cody. He knew about the character assassination and he was aware that Nathan had carefully engineered things by lying and distorting the truth over a long period of time to convince the other two board members of his distorted view.

But as the victim, Harvey was now in a 'lose-lose' situation. If he told Todd the truth, it would be playing into the hands of Nathan. Having prepared the ground by assassinating Harvey's character to Todd, Nathan had made it impossible for Harvey to tell Todd the truth without appearing to be envious himself. As a result of the meeting, Todd was now under the impression that Harvey was incompetent, so if Harvey told Todd that Nathan was a liar, although this was true, it would appear that he was trying to cover his own inadequacies. But if Harvey said nothing, Nathan would have achieved his aim of undermining him and placing himself in the position whereby he could take the credit for the company's successes.

This should, in Nathan's eyes, result in him receiving admiration from others, primarily those he set out to impress. Engineering the receipt of admiration is obsessive and compulsive, and essential to maintaining the narcissist's false image. The fact that Nathan would be taking most or all of the credit for something to which he had contributed little was irrelevant to him. It would have the desired effect of taking him back to his days as a child, when his parents did everything for him, putting him on a pedestal, and over-praising him. It is only narcissists who feel entitled to special treatment and privileges without ever having earned them.

Although character assassination appears on the face of it an aggressive action, in truth it is defensive. In fact, Nathan and Cody used character assassination as a defence mechanism, which pre-supposes that they were victims, fighting for survival. In some respects this was true – they *were* fighting for survival. Nathan was only able to survive by projecting a false image of himself to others, including Todd. The continuing success of the business, over which Nathan had almost no input, meant that he was now perilously close to having his image exposed as a sham. Narcissists can only survive with their false image intact, and they will go to any lengths to protect it. Cody, on the other hand, relied on the protection offered by Nathan, without which his own survival was also threatened.

Who is the Victim?

'An organization ideal is a narcissistic fantasy. The only question is who ultimately gets to be the narcissist.'[5]

The following statement is one of many made about Harvey at the meeting when Nathan and Cody assassinated Harvey's character in the eyes of Todd: 'He lost the system that just transfers internal emails.' The statement simply suggests incompetence on behalf of Harvey, the person who lost the system that transfers internal emails. But if a malignant narcissist says it, there is almost certainly more to it than meets the eye.

First, if we analyse the veracity of the statement we find that it is not true: Harvey did not lose the system that transfers internal emails. Second, if we are now able to get an understanding of Nathan's motive behind the statement, we find that there is no incompetence to be found in relation to the narcissist's intended victim, but rather that it is Nathan himself who is either incompetent in relation to the subject matter, or feels incompetent.

The only element of the statement made by Nathan that had some basis in fact is the piece of information that the system that transfers the emails did break down. When the system, a computer system with a server at the hub, was installed some months earlier at the head office, an IT consultant set up the server to store the emails. He liaised with Harvey during the installation of the system, solely because Harvey was the only director at the site with IT knowledge; Nathan and Cody's knowledge in relation to IT was very limited. This was at the root of the problem. Although Harvey's knowledge of IT was not great either, Nathan envied Harvey because he knew more than him; he was superior to him in this respect, and narcissists abhor feeling inferior.

The truth in relation to what happened was known by Nathan, Cody and Harvey, but not by Todd. No fault for the problem could be attributed to Harvey, but as Harvey was not present at the meeting, Nathan and Cody believed that they were in a position to lie without being found out.

What happened in reality was as follows: When the IT consultant originally set up the server, he should have set a limit to the storage capacity of emails such that when a specified amount of hard disk space was used, the oldest emails were deleted; but he didn't do this. The emails continued to be stored until the hard disk on the server was full and everything ground to a halt. In fact, it transpired that the problem had been greatly exacerbated by Nathan, who had received a deluge of pornographic emails after registering his company email address with a pornography website.

The server problem happened one morning when Harvey was at one of the company's branches. When he arrived back at the head office just before lunch, he found that Nathan was animated. The staff had turned to Nathan to resolve the problem as the company at that time did not have IT support staff to call on, but his lack of IT knowledge meant that he was unable to do anything. It appeared that he felt impotent and frustrated, possibly at a lost opportunity to impress others in the office.

The problem was evidently beyond Nathan's limited IT knowledge, but it was also beyond Harvey's knowledge. However, Harvey telephoned a contact, who came over and solved the problem. Before leaving, Harvey's contact explained to the three directors who were located at the head office site – Harvey, Nathan and Cody – what had happened, and said he wouldn't charge the company for his time. So the problem was fixed soon after Harvey's arrival and at no charge to the company. Not only did Nathan feel inferior, but even worse, he knew that the managers and staff whom he continually tried to impress also saw what had happened, which made him feel that he was inferior in their eyes too. This is the worst of all situations for a narcissist. The managers and staff in the head office probably didn't care one way or the other, they were just happy that the computers were working again; but to the narcissist, it's all about perception.

For Nathan to tell Todd that Harvey had lost the system that transfers internal emails, knowing that it was untrue, was either an act of malice or an attempt to purge himself of his intense envious feelings and protect his false image so as to avoid the danger of feeling anxious and stressed. In reality it was probably a combination of the two. A malignant narcissist will not shrink from any level of malice or evil to lessen his negative emotional feelings and to protect his false image.

But the question still remains: who was the victim? Harvey certainly felt like a victim – he felt that he had been stabbed in the back, having had this lie and many others told about him without him even being present, not just by Nathan, the narcissist, but with the full support of Cody, the codependent director whom he had considered to be both a colleague and a good friend. But Nathan and Cody also clearly felt like victims. Nathan, as a narcissist, did what narcissists always do – he defended the image that he constantly projected to the outside world from someone – Harvey in this case – whose very presence was a constant reminder of his feelings of inadequacy and worthlessness. Cody's unequivocal support for Nathan was as a result of his codependency.

To the narcissist this defence is a matter of the utmost importance. It's easy to understand why when you consider that his alternative is to admit to himself his inferiority in relation to Harvey, and thus succumb to feelings of inadequacy, worthlessness, anxiety, stress, despair and fear, and potentially also a period of deep depression. Nathan felt that Harvey had shown him up in the eyes of the managers and staff in the head office, so he felt like a victim. Cody, who felt a compelling need to lie in support of his narcissistic colleague, also felt like a victim, having been used by Nathan; the alternative for Cody would have been to support Harvey, but then risk the almost certain withdrawal of Nathan's support, leaving him feeling defenceless against Nathan's wrath and against a perceived threat from Harvey; although Cody was not actually threatened by Harvey, Nathan's paranoia would have convinced him that he was.

But from a philosophical viewpoint, should Harvey have been more considerate of the feelings of Nathan and Cody? After all, it was Harvey's behaviour that resulted in them resorting to character assassination, as a potent defence mechanism. If Harvey hadn't returned and resolved the problem with the server it would have been left to Nathan to resolve the problem, which he surely would have done eventually. There would have been a cost to the company in terms of time lost with the computers being offline, and potentially also the cost of calling out an IT consultant to resolve the problem, but it would have resulted in a boost to Nathan's self-esteem.

Repressed emotions are forced into the unconscious at an early age due to emotional abuse, along with suppressed emotions. The difference is that repressed emotions never enter consciousness, whereas suppressed emotions do. They are all emotions that we were not able to deal with, so they have been either consciously or subconsciously denied, and end up in the unconscious part of the mind where they don't make us feel uncomfortable.

Unfortunately, triggers in the form of words or action from others can bring these painful feelings back into the conscious. We don't know why we feel uncomfortable, as we cannot usually make the connection between the painful feelings and what caused them earlier in life.

The vast majority of these feelings have been caused by our parents who, usually inadvertently, have used us, their children, to get rid of painful feelings of their own, probably caused by their parents. The problems get passed down from one generation to the next.

The narcissist has suffered in this way much more than the normal adult, as he has had a narcissistic parent, so his reactions are so much more pronounced. His need to get rid of the painful feelings triggered by others becomes overriding. This happens naturally through repression, nature's way of dealing with problems the mind can't deal with. The painful feelings are moved to the unconscious mind, where they are forgotten; at least until they are triggered later.

If nature doesn't deal with the problem, the narcissist can achieve a similar result by conscious denial – by simply denying to himself that it is a problem – by suppressing it. The painful feelings are again moved, but this time to the subconscious mind, where they are forgotten; but not entirely – they remain accessible when called upon or, as before, when they are triggered later. This appears to have been how Nathan dealt with his inferiority feelings in relation to Harvey. But the problem built up over a period of time because Harvey, the person supplying the triggers, was continually in Nathan's environment in the workplace, so Nathan's painful feelings were recurring over and over again.

After denial, the next stage of defence is normally lies and distortions, then projection; the narcissist will resort to projecting his painful feelings directly back onto the person who triggered them. But if this strategy also fails, he will enlist one or more of his codependent friends to help him discharge his painful emotions, knowing that they will support his distorted view. Codependent characters, such as Cody, already have strong depressive traits and have been trained from birth to respond to narcissists' behaviour and recognise their feelings. So they unconsciously take over and enact the depressive components of their narcissistic associate.

Now the narcissist and his trusted codependent friend have a common enemy – in this case, Harvey. When projection fails to rid the narcissist of his painful feelings, as it inevitably will after repeated attempts over a long period due to the law of diminishing returns, the next stage in the quest to rid the narcissist of his pain, now also felt by his trusted codependent sidekick, is the character assassination of the person who has been causing those painful feelings.

Nathan followed this sequence of denial, lies and distortion, projection, manipulation of his trusted codependent friend, and then use of character assassination. Harvey was the target.

It may be that by denying Nathan the opportunity to deal with the problem while those he wanted to admire him looked on, Harvey supplied a trigger that brought Nathan's repressed or suppressed emotions from his unconscious and subconscious mind into consciousness. Such intense feelings of frustration may have been felt by him much earlier in his life when, for example, a parent would not let him do things for himself. These situations are not uncommon. They result from narcissistic parents who use their children as a tool to give them the admiration they crave – for instance, saying to their child, 'You have no idea, you're useless; watch me son, I'll show you how it's done.' And when the child becomes an adult he uses the same parental behaviour to assuage his own painful feelings. The parent effectively taught the child how to deal with the painful feelings that he had caused. So when someone like Harvey comes along and shows the narcissist 'how it's done', it triggers the painful feelings he felt earlier in life.

But if Nathan consciously denied to himself the suppressed painful feelings that were experienced in dealing with his feelings of inferiority by his subconscious mind, where they remained accessible when called upon, it suggests that part, if not all, of his malicious behaviour towards Harvey was deliberate. Only repressed painful feelings move to the unconscious, out of the mind's awareness. It is highly likely that in this case Nathan consciously suppressed his painful feelings in relation to Harvey, moving them to his subconscious.

The difference between Harvey's behaviour and that of Nathan was always clearly defined during work. Harvey's primary consideration when making decisions was based on what was best for the company, as it was in this case. However, Nathan's primary consideration when making decisions was based on what was best for him, taking into consideration opportunities for boosts to his self-esteem and, in particular, opportunities that allowed him to avoid emotional pain. If Harvey had been more sensitive to Nathan's emotional pain, perhaps Nathan would not have felt so much like a victim. And perhaps he may not have had to use his defence mechanisms such as distortion and projection so extensively if there had not been the triggers that Harvey constantly supplied by putting the company first, often in conflict with the unconscious drive of Nathan's ego.

And the question that also needs to be asked is this: Did Harvey perhaps put the company first as a cover to enable him to resolve problems such as, in this case, the failure of the server? By doing so, there was the potential for him to gain admiration from others to feed his own narcissistic needs. On the other hand, if Harvey's primary consideration was the company as opposed to his own emotional needs, it suggests that any narcissism that may have been evident in his behaviour was 'healthy narcissism'.

But it would be wrong to ignore Harvey's contribution to Nathan's malevolent and at times malicious behaviour towards him. As CEO, he was not a passive observer of the developments leading up to his character assassination by Nathan and Cody.

The Story behind Harvey's 'Speech'

'Many people suffer all their lives from this oppressive feeling of guilt, the sense of not having lived up to their parents' expectations.'[6]

Another of Nathan's statements to Todd, the fourth director, about Harvey when he wasn't present was: 'It's only two or three weeks ago he spent about eight days preparing for that f***ing speech at Alton Towers.' The expletive shows the strength of feeling felt by Nathan, but his conscious mind was probably not aware of why his feelings were running so high. The statement is most probably heavily loaded with Nathan's past history relating to his father.

Despite Harvey knowing Nathan for many years, Nathan never discussed his father with him; in fact, he never mentioned his father at all. It is well established that narcissists rarely, if ever, discuss their past history in relation to family life. However, Harvey had been told that Nathan's father worked at fairgrounds and theme parks. As Alton Towers is a major theme park in England, there is likely to be a strong connection between the narcissist's repressed memory relating to his father and Harvey's activity.

First, we need to know if the statement made by Nathan was true. The answer, as before, is no, although also as before, there is an element of the statement that relates to an actual occurrence. Harvey had been invited by the UK Health and Safety Executive, a government body, to give a presentation in relation to the type of work carried out by the company and how it contributes to the safety of the rides at fairgrounds and theme parks. He prepared a PowerPoint presentation one weekend and took it into the office on Monday morning, ironically to consult Nathan on one or two points regarding fairgrounds and theme parks about which he wasn't sure.

The time spent on the presentation that morning was no more than two or three hours, but in any case, due to its potential for generating sales, the time was justified. This presents a second causal possibility relating to Nathan's statement. Nathan was responsible for sales within the organisation, and Harvey's presentation at Alton

Towers had the potential to generate sales for the company. It was common knowledge in the company that Nathan was not proactive in obtaining new sales. Again, there is likely to be a strong connection between Nathan's repressed memories and Harvey's activity that reminded Nathan of intense feelings of inferiority, failure and worthlessness from his childhood.

Once more, it points to the probability that the roots of Nathan's problems lie in having had one or two emotionally insecure parents who depended on him, their child, to maintain their equilibrium. A child responds intuitively to his parents' needs, developing an unconscious state that responds to the needs of others.

The malignancy in a malignant narcissist is developed during childhood and adolescence when a parent who is a malignant narcissist continues to use the child to maintain his equilibrium by denigrating him when he feels triggers from his own unconscious mind, caused by his own emotionally abused and neglected childhood. The denigrated child represses these intense feelings of inferiority, failure and worthlessness which then reappear through triggers to their unconscious mind in adult life. As the triggers come from feelings that have been repressed, it isn't possible to make any connection between the feelings and their parents who caused them to be repressed in the first place.

Harvey was doing exactly the kind of work that Nathan would have dearly loved to do – technical sales work associated with fairgrounds and theme parks, with the potential for receiving admiration from an audience. It is highly likely that the theme park stirred memories in Nathan of his father, whom he would have wanted to impress, and the potential for admiration is something that narcissists crave most, if not all, of their waking hours. But Nathan's fear of failure, most likely as a result of an emotionally abused childhood, had prevented him from gaining the necessary confidence and achieving the required qualifications to do what Harvey was doing. Pathological envy is the almost inevitable outcome for the narcissistic personality, and it would typically manifest itself in a vitriolic verbal attack on the object of his envy, as it did in this case.

Again, it could be argued that we should not ignore Harvey's contribution to Nathan's malevolent behaviour towards him. Harvey was aware of Nathan's neurotic and narcissistic behaviour, and he was aware that Nathan's father worked at fairgrounds and theme parks, yet he accepted the request to talk on the subject from the Heath and Safety Executive, and also involved Nathan in his preparation for the talk. The philosophical question behind Harvey's behaviour is: 'How accountable should a CEO be held for managing the behaviour of psychologically damaged managers who work under him?' The answer to this question is outside the scope of this book.

The Story Behind Harvey's Holidays

'To judge correctly is to affirm an object if it exists or to deny an object if it does not exist. To judge incorrectly is to affirm an object that does not exist or to deny an object that does exist.'[7]

Another deprecating statement made by Nathan about Harvey was: 'He's taken that many f***ing Fridays off.' Again the expletive shows the strength of feeling felt by Nathan. As in the preceding analyses, to understand him we need to assess the veracity of the statement and then look into the story behind it to identify the reasons why Nathan exhibited so much anger towards Harvey.

As is usual with assertions made by a malignant narcissist, there is a kernel of truth in the statement. Harvey had taken two Fridays off as official holidays during the previous three months, which he was wholly entitled to do. The statement made by Nathan was both crude and vitriolic, and it implied behaviour by Harvey that was unfair or unreasonable, suggesting that Harvey had taken 'many' days off. Yet the fact that he had taken just two days off as holiday could not possibly be the sole cause of the underlying hostility shown by Nathan in his statement – someone taking two days' holiday over a three-month period can hardly in itself be construed as antagonistic, and designed by Harvey to intimidate Nathan.

The triggers felt by Nathan were most likely twofold, and both would be impossible to identify without knowledge of Nathan's history. The first one relates to Nathan's prior academic failures, and the other relates to Nathan's own record of taking holidays and other time off. When Nathan mirrored himself against Harvey in both of these respects, his unconscious most likely triggered feelings of inferiority in relation to Harvey, connected to repressed emotions relating to failure during his childhood and early adulthood, and possibly to suppressed emotions in later life.

Looking at Nathan's academic record first, it reveals that he did not hold any higher education qualifications – his academic study ceased when he left school. However, Harvey held a university degree. Harvey overheard Nathan talking to someone on the phone, discussing individuals they knew who had been to university and gained degrees. What Nathan said during the course of the lengthy conversation was revealing. At one point he said that he had gone to grammar school and that his four best friends had all gone on to either Oxford or Cambridge University. If this was true, the fact that he never progressed to higher education suggests that he may have feelings of resentment and failure in relation to the academic achievements of others who are or were significant in his life. If Nathan studied at school with his four best friends who all went on to university, there must have been an expectation from his parents that he would also go to university. As a result, it is probable that his parents showed him their disappointment at his academic failure. So one trigger that may have prompted Nathan's venomous verbal attack on Harvey was that Nathan knew that Harvey had spent the two days' holiday doing research at a university library, working towards a postgraduate degree.

A further point that may be revealing is that during the telephone conversation, despite mentioning numerous individuals he appeared to know who held university degrees, Nathan didn't mention

Harvey, his colleague and co-director. In fact, Nathan had never acknowledged that Harvey even held a university degree. This behaviour – 'denying the object' – is recognised in psychology as a defence used to deny someone deserved recognition, usually as a result of a narcissist's pathological envy. Typically, the narcissist (or the codependent who supports the narcissist's world view) will take every opportunity to deny the importance of the envied target.

The unconscious triggers felt by Nathan in relation to the taking of holidays may not only relate to repressed emotions from child-hood, but may also hark back to more recent suppressed emotions from early adulthood that have entered his consciousness. In order to deal with the painful feelings evoked in adolescence or early adulthood, he has suppressed them, in contrast to the repressed painful emotional feelings felt very early in life that have never entered consciousness. So again, when Nathan mirrored himself against Harvey in relation to holidays and time taken off, he will have felt bad about himself due to the large amount of time he had taken off work, mostly unrecorded.

Over a number of years Harvey didn't take his full holiday enti-tlement, accumulating over seventy days that he never took. On one occasion Nathan found himself in a position whereby although he wanted to take family holidays, he felt that he was not able to record them; the reason was that even though he was entitled to the holidays, taking them would have had the effect of making him feel inferior to Harvey, with his superior holiday record. Feelings of inferiority in narcissists are unconsciously triggered from past his-tories, but since Nathan desperately did not want to feel inferior to Harvey, he found a typically narcissistic answer to his problem.

Nathan took a holiday with his wife and family at a resort over eighty miles away. It is likely that he told his wife that he was too important to be able to take the time off, so he would have to check daily at work to make sure that everything was all right, and make sure that his staff knew what to do. Thus he had the excuse to drive back from holiday each morning and call in to the office for about ten minutes, then return to the holiday resort. This had the effect of maintaining a grandiose image in the eyes of his wife and family, and at the same time gave him an excuse not to record his time off as official holiday time.

Nathan's malicious statement about Harvey again contained a kernel of truth: Harvey had indeed taken two Fridays off work. But without stating the number of days taken, by merely saying, 'He's taken that many f***ing Fridays off', Nathan made it sound to Todd as though Harvey had taken many more days off than he really had, and by saying that Harvey had taken the days off but omitting to say that they were holidays, he implied that the days off had been taken illicitly. This suggested that Harvey was taking days off without recording them, when in fact the only person who had taken days off without recording them was Nathan himself. Again, Nathan was using projection as a means of getting rid of his unwanted painful feelings.

Why Did Nathan Lie?

> *'They f*** you up, your mum and dad.*
> *They may not mean to, but they do.*
> *They fill you with the faults they had*
> *And add some extra, just for you.'*[8]

Alice Miller, in her book *The Drama of the Gifted Child*,[9] described how the roots of narcissism can be found very early in life due to the impact an insecure mother can have on her child. Alice Miller wasn't the first person to notice this; nearly two and a half thousand years ago, Plato explained how harmful ideas are sometimes implanted in us by others whom we trust, such as our parents, when we are young and vulnerable. These ideas then exert undesirable controls over us, but we defend them all the same because we erroneously believe they are our own.[10]

In later life this insecurity can manifest itself in a number of ways. The adult will have to deal with the repressed emotions that exist in the unconscious, which act as triggers relating to the repressed painful memories. He may become an extrovert, for example, and develop a 'need to achieve', or an introvert, and develop other defence mechanisms such as living for others, feeling responsible for them and attempting to regulate the world around them. The extrovert tends to become narcissistic and the introvert tends to become codependent.

The insecure adult who develops a narcissistic need to achieve feels a compelling need to push himself forward as a result of the traumas he suffered when young, constantly trying to prove that he is not a failure, but unaware why he feels this compelling need to succeed. His desire is to satisfy an internal need for achievement. But if he externalises this need, instead of driving himself forward to achieve in a narcissistic but healthy way, he manipulates others to admire him in order to satisfy his emotional needs, in a narcissistic and unhealthy way.

Externalisation of the need to achieve by the narcissistic child can lead to him growing into an adult malignant narcissist. In order for this externalisation to happen, he needs input from his parents or carers, one of whom will be narcissistic. When the child or young adult succeeds at something, his parents put him on a pedestal and over-praise him, making him feel entitled to special treatment and privileges without the need to earn them. When he fails, however, he is vilified, denigrated by his narcissistic parent. This results in the child or young adult feeling that he can't control his own life. He feels that he has to rely on others – more significant others, such as his father.

But this creates a conflict. Whilst the young adult feels as though he isn't in control of his life, he also feels entitled to special treatment and privileges without the need to earn them. How can anyone obtain the special treatment and privileges that he feels he is entitled to when he doesn't feel in control of his own life? The answer is that he uses significant others to obtain them for him. This acts as a substitute for the feelings he used to experience when he was put on a pedestal by his parents. By manipulating, or controlling, others, he can return to the childhood feelings he so enjoyed when being praised and admired.

The adolescent's failure to impress his narcissistic parent was inevitable as the parent felt he must remain superior, as do all narcissists. So the adolescent had to deal with the resulting negative emotions brought about by feeling that he had failed and that he was inferior – something that adolescents are not well equipped to do without at least one supportive parent. This is how the malignant narcissist is created in early adulthood.

All denigrating statements made by a malignant narcissist about his victim have a story behind them. It's just a matter of understanding the history, the qualities or the possessions of the victim in order to identify the reason why the narcissist feels inferior, and of understanding the current circumstances in order to recognise the trigger.

We know that the malignant narcissist's negative feelings are the result of repressed or suppressed emotions that have been stored from earlier in his life, and which are being awakened in later life but without the original connection ever becoming clear. In this case, the underlying problem that caused Nathan to lie behind Harvey's back was most likely caused many years before Nathan and Harvey had even met.

Harvey was a 'significant other' to Nathan, who hated being in an environment where others, including Todd, acknowledged Harvey's success as CEO. Nathan's desire was to obtain the special treatment and privileges to which he felt he was entitled. In order to achieve that aim he needed to be in control, but he saw Harvey as an obstacle. He felt that he needed to remove the obstacle, but he was unable to attack Harvey on the basis of his record as CEO because it was clear that Harvey had been successful over a long period, despite Nathan's ongoing attempts to undermine him. And he also could not attack Harvey's personal integrity, as Harvey's impeccable behaviour did not allow him to.

So Nathan's venomous attacks were not aimed directly at Harvey, as he was not vulnerable, and possibly also because Nathan feared that he would respond to any such attacks by pointing out Nathan's own inadequacies and lack of integrity; instead, Nathan lied and distorted the facts behind Harvey's back to those he wanted to impress. This had the benefit of boosting his self-esteem in two ways – by allowing him to feel that he was taking control of the situation, and by dint of denigrating his prey.

Nathan appeared to be an insecure adult because of the traumas he had suffered when young. As a result, he wanted to be admired by others who were significant to him, including Harvey, and constantly tried to prove that he was not a failure in the only way he knew how – by manipulating others. But the one person significant to him whom he was unable to manipulate was Harvey, so in an attempt to achieve his aims, he lied behind Harvey's back.

The damage done to Nathan's character by lying is apparent through his narcissistic behaviour, and is perhaps best summed up by quotations from two of the greatest philosophers. Plato said, 'False words are not only evil in themselves, but they infect the soul with evil.' And Immanuel Kant said, 'By a lie, a man ... annihilates his dignity as a man.'

How Should We Treat a Malignant Narcissist?

'If we are considerate of those who are not considerate of us, we may be ethically exploited, or worse.'[11]

There is little doubt that Nathan's problems related to his feeling of inferiority in relation to Harvey. Although Harvey spent time trying to help Nathan by assisting him in obtaining various vocational qualifications, showing him how to use his computer, and doing many of the technical aspects of Nathan's job that Nathan couldn't do because he didn't hold the necessary qualifications, Nathan still hated Harvey and denigrated him at every opportunity. By helping Nathan, Harvey only made the problem worse, as being helped made Nathan feel even more inferior, triggering those negative feelings from his unconscious.

Nathan fits perfectly into the a category of individuals who live under the illusion that they are entitled to be served and who care little about hurting and exploiting others in the pursuit of their own advancement. Whilst Harvey was considerate of Nathan, Nathan was not considerate of Harvey in return. As a result, Harvey laid himself open to being exploited, which Nathan made the most of over a number of years, culminating in ruthless character assassination.

Harvey knew that Nathan was constantly stabbing him in the back, yet continued to try and help him whenever he needed it. Was this naivety on Harvey's part? Harvey argued that if he responded to Nathan by fighting fire with fire, he would simply be lowering himself to the same level as Nathan. Harvey's strategy worked for a number of years; the company at which he was CEO prospered despite Nathan's self-serving behaviour, although Harvey believed that it would have been much more successful without Nathan's negative influence.

There were occasions when Nathan's behaviour – putting his ego needs before the needs of the company – was very costly to the company. For example, on one occasion the company won what was its biggest and most profitable contract since its formation. It was potentially long term and involved working to nuclear requirements. When challenged on a technical point by a senior engineer at the company, Nathan refused to back down even though he was clearly wrong. He appeared to be putting his ego first and the business second.

The technical point related to an instruction given by Nathan to the senior engineer that deviated from the correct interpretation of the nuclear procedure. Any change from the procedure could have huge implications from a safety point of view, and when an inspector from the nuclear company noticed this deviation, he challenged Nathan. Again, Nathan refused to acknowledge that he was wrong, despite clear evidence to the contrary. His refusal to back down in the face of overwhelming evidence against him resulted in the company losing the contract and being banned from future nuclear work. It lost the biggest and most profitable contract it had ever had.

Nathan denied any wrongdoing; instead he blamed the inspector from the nuclear company, repeating over and over to anyone and everyone who mentioned the subject that the inspector had an ulterior motive – that he wanted to move the work to another company with which he had a relationship. This was completely untrue, but it was the only way that Nathan could deal with his feelings of failure – through projecting his feelings onto the inspector from the nuclear company, someone who was entirely innocent.

Getting rid of his feelings of shame is a narcissist's overriding need. His negative feelings must be projected onto someone else, as the alternative is to have feelings of anxiety, even despair, possibly leading to a period of depression. He needs to re-establish his credibility in the eyes of those who feed his ego's needs.

A significant psychological difficulty that Nathan may have had was that the senior inspector had consulted Harvey on the technical point, and Harvey had agreed with him. Harvey then told Nathan that he agreed with the senior inspector, rather than with him. Nathan's refusal to admit to the nuclear inspector that he was wrong may have been related to Harvey's assertion the previous day that he was indeed wrong. To admit it at this stage would, in effect, mean Nathan admitting that he was inferior to Harvey. Having invested so much political capital in convincing others of his superiority and at the same time taking every opportunity to denigrate Harvey, climbing down would have meant losing face. Nathan felt that his ego simply had to take precedence, even with so much at stake for the company.

Even after such a major setback, Harvey continued to be considerate towards Nathan. He didn't take the opportunity to denigrate him in the presence of others; he succeeded in getting the ban by the nuclear company lifted without using Nathan as a scapegoat, which would have been the easier solution. But the consideration shown by

Harvey for Nathan appeared to have the effect of making Nathan despise him all the more.

There are a number of alternative courses of action that one can take when confronted with a malignant narcissist such as Nathan, one of which is appeasement, letting him have his way. This is the course taken by codependents such as Cody. You let the narcissist win, be nice to him, on the basis that he will be kind to you when you are completely under his control. This worked for Cody, in that Nathan looked after him, but it ultimately meant that Cody lost a good friend in Harvey. He also suffered a blow to his self-esteem after being sucked into Nathan's world of lies, distortion and projection, and then being found out by Harvey.

Neville Chamberlain, Prime Minister of the United Kingdom from 1937 to 1940, tried appeasement when attempting to deal with the threat of Germany's leader Adolf Hitler. He signed the Munich Agreement in 1938 conceding the Sudetenland region of Czechoslovakia to Germany. But as Sir Winston Churchill said, 'An appeaser is one who feeds a crocodile, hoping it will eat him last.' When appeasement failed, Chamberlain tried containment, restraining the malignant narcissist's ambitions in 1939. That also failed, ending in the United Kingdom declaring war on Germany later that year.

Another course of action that one can take when confronted with a malignant narcissist is the defensive tactic – that used by Harvey against Nathan. Harvey didn't react to Nathan's malevolent behaviour towards him, he simply dealt with the problems Nathan caused, and challenged him when necessary. This method worked for a time. Not challenging him on every occasion when he behaved badly and only challenging him when needed had the effect of stopping Nathan getting over-confident and, as a consequence, it stopped him from getting over-aggressive in carrying out his malevolent acts.

The difficulty when challenging a malignant narcissist is that he always responds with lies and distortion. Even when proven wrong conclusively, if he doesn't simply walk away, he will continue to lie and distort, and project if necessary, for as long as it takes until he reaches a position where the person challenging him is not able to prove he is lying. At this point the malignant narcissist claims victory. Nathan adopted this strategy on many occasions when confronted by Harvey. Despite these problems, Harvey's way of dealing with him was moderately successful over a number of years, but ultimately it failed. Harvey showed restraint and staying power, and achieved moderate success for the company in the face of such malevolent behaviour driven by Nathan's acute paranoia and pathological envy, but the malignant narcissist will always win eventually, as he can never give up. If his opponent is not another malignant narcissist, but is someone who refuses to fight fire with fire, the malignant narcissist will continue fighting for as long as it takes to win, using his entire armoury of psychological defences to ensure that his false image remains intact.

The only option available for Harvey to overcome Nathan was for him to use retaliatory tactics, to fight fire with fire, going on the offensive and destroying his false image. It would involve exposing Nathan to others, including all of his codependent supporters, in such a way as to shame him to the core. This would have the effect of driving him into deep despair and possibly a period of depression if he was not able to convince the significant others in his life to believe his world view. It could also have the effect of eliciting a violent, aggressive response from Nathan.

But Harvey was not prepared to do this. By remaining considerate of Nathan despite his malicious and at times evil behaviour towards him, Harvey was able to maintain his own relatively healthy emotional state. Maintaining the moral high ground, even when he was being lied about behind his back, helped preserve his healthy self-esteem. Harvey knew that to engage in retaliatory tactics to destroy Nathan would leave him feeling bad about himself, and so, in effect, end up wearing Nathan's shoes.

8

Trust and Loyalty

Can You Trust a Narcissist or a Codependent?

Trust is the expectation/belief that another party will take one's own interests into account in their actions.

Mistrust and suspicion have spread across all areas of life, not least due to the increasing influence of narcissists and their codependents. Narcissists are attracted to political office, and citizens no longer trust politicians. But citizens' trust of doctors, journalists and those working in many other professions that used to be respected is now also falling. Loss of trust increasingly characterises contemporary society.

Trust is important; it is the glue that holds society as we know it together. It arrived relatively late in the evolution of man. First, man became able to make predictions about the behaviour of others, and once trust became possible, interactions could be sustained that would otherwise collapse, thus enhancing the quality of cooperation, and weaving the fabric of society together.

Trust arises through cooperation, but it relies on memory. If you do someone a favour, they remember it and return it at a later time. It is reciprocal altruism: 'You scratch my back and I'll scratch yours.' The human mind is able to form a representation of what is going on in the other person's mind, and then relate it back to its own interests.

Trust begins to break down when the narcissistic tendencies of some members of the team start to influence decision making. The team members could be, for example, a husband and wife, a business or society as a whole. Those who have been brought up as trusting individuals are most at risk. For a narcissist to be successful, he is completely dependent upon others trusting him. Once he has established what the other party believes to be a trusting relationship, the narcissist then has the power to exploit. As Professor Lou Marinoff, in his book, *The Big Questions: How Philosophy Can Change Your Life* said, 'if we are considerate of those who are not considerate of us, we may be ethically exploited, or worse.'

A trusting relationship requires tolerance, the ability to give the benefit of the doubt, particularly when the situation gets confused through interruptions, chatter or other people's views. But in these situations the narcissist is at his most dangerous and exploitative. The more the narcissist is tolerated, the more he gains in confidence, and the better he is able to establish his base. The longer he is tolerated, the more difficult it is for the victim or victims to escape.

The capacity for trust and the capacity for mistrust go hand in hand. Often very little information is required to place trust in someone – first impressions or appearances can often be accurate, but they can also be subject to our prejudices.

Some people are systematically suspicious or gullible – they can't place trust or mistrust with intelligence. As stated in Chapter 2, a self-confessed narcissist once said, 'One feels ill at ease in the presence of a narcissist for no apparent reason.' But for most of us, feeling ill at ease is not sufficient justification to mistrust someone, particularly if that person has had a third-party validation. And this is precisely how narcissists work.

The narcissist is aware more than anyone that a third-party validation gives him the credibility he needs to gain the trust of others. For example, a narcissist who has failed academically may vicariously acquire the admiration he craves by marrying a professor or a doctor. Narcissists invariably go to great lengths to associate themselves with people of high status.

We have already seen that the glue that holds all the pieces in place for an effective and efficient team is trust. Whether a team is a family, a sports team or a board of directors, success is dependent upon there being sufficient trust between the team members to enable it to operate.

And we have also established in Chapter 7 that the answer to the question of whether you can trust a narcissist or codependent in a team situation is a resounding no. The narcissist and his codependent in the example given lied, denied and distorted facts whenever they found themselves in what they perceived as a threatening situation.

It is necessary to have trust in society for it to function well – it falls apart without it. The benefit of trust is that it reduces transaction costs. If we trust someone, we don't need to draw up a contract between us. But a balanced society also needs a healthy amount of distrust, such that a system of checks and balances is developed. It's by exploiting this need for trust in relationships, at work, and in society in general that the narcissist is able to be so successful.

We may be able to learn something from the Stoics. One of the guiding principles of Stoicism[1] is not to overvalue anything that can be taken away from you by others, as by doing so you place yourself in their power. Thus, placing too much trust in a narcissist is potentially a very dangerous thing to do. Unfortunately, codependents do this as a matter of course; it is the basis of their relationship with the narcissist, and the method by which the narcissist is frequently able to exert complete control over them.

This is how it works: Codependents feel insecure; they don't trust their own judgement because they have been brought up by parents or carers who made all of the decisions for them. Typical codependents need an authority figure to make the decisions for them, someone they can trust, a parent figure. The narcissist presents himself as a paternal figure, the image of a confident decision maker, someone who can be trusted. His offer to the codependent is 'you trust me and I will look after you'. They are attracted to each other; the narcissist gets the power he yearns for, which gives him the feeling of control in his life, and the codependent gets the security she yearns for.

These relationships may be husband and wife or boyfriend and girlfriend, where either one can be the narcissist (though more often than not the narcissist is the man), or may be same sex relationships. In all cases, the relationship is conditional on the codependent helping the narcissist meet his or her personal needs, such as sex, status, financial support or social opportunities.[2]

In the business environment, this relationship can be between a manager and an employee, where the manager looks after his employee so long as the employee covers up for him whenever necessary. Once the manager has 'hooked' his codependent employee, the employee then finds himself in positions where he has to cover up for the unpredictable behaviour of his narcissistic manager. As he feels responsible for him, he tries to regulate the world around him.

If you look around you there are likely to be many examples of codependents covering for their narcissistic partners, bosses and friends. Charlotte was an office manager whose boss was a malignant narcissist. The boss used vulgar language on a regular basis during the working day. So whenever Charlotte interviewed potential office workers, usually female, she always asked them if they would mind her swearing, despite the fact that she didn't swear herself. She was taking on the responsibility for her boss's behaviour.

Another example is that of Emily, who had a husband who used to embarrass her in front of her friends and relatives by undermining her confidence, telling her she was ugly, stupid, and so on to the point where sometimes she would have to leave, usually in tears. She would later excuse his behaviour by saying, 'He's nice really. It's my fault, I get so emotional.'

The codependent wife or employee trusts her husband or manager implicitly, and so becomes reliant on the security he offers. This may be through the process of paternal or maternal transference.[3] Unfortunately for the codependent wife or employee, the narcissist knows how much his codependent partner needs him and at the same time fears him; he knows that there is always an implicit threat that he will withdraw his security. It is this paranoid fear felt by the codependent that enables the narcissist to exert complete control over her. The codependent has made the fundamental error of overvaluing something that can be taken away from her.

How Loyal is a Narcissist?

'Unless you can find some sort of loyalty, you cannot find unity and peace in your active living.'[4]

Loyalty is a means of resolving fear and developing trust, and loyalty to others means putting their needs above your own, and trusting that your needs will be supported in due time. As we now know, codependents trust their narcissistic husband (or wife) or manager and they are subsequently loyal to them; but is that loyalty reciprocated? Will the codependent's needs be supported in due time?

In the home, narcissists demand loyalty, not to their family but to themselves. This results in dysfunctional family relationships. If any other family member tries to take centre stage, the narcissist quickly puts them back in their place. It is the same in the workplace. Narcissistic bosses demand loyalty from their subordinates, but loyalty to the business takes a distant second place. If it is a choice between the business going into liquidation or the avoidance of damage to the narcissist's ego, the narcissist will always choose avoidance of damage to his ego.

Robert, a narcissistic sales director, needed to clear his office on a Friday afternoon for the painters and decorators to work over the weekend. He had three managers working in the next office, Alan, George and James, so he told them to move the office furniture out. James refused as he had an urgent job that had to be done by the end of the day for an important client. Robert accused him of being disloyal and of not being a team worker. In fact, the manager was showing true loyalty to the company by making sure that an important customer was looked after.

On another occasion Robert had the choice between attending a meeting where he may have been able to win back a major customer whom the company had just lost, or meeting with fellow directors to discuss company cars. Despite being the sales director, he chose to attend the meeting about company cars. He clearly demonstrated that his loyalty to his own agenda was over and above that of the company.

A narcissistic father will demand complete loyalty from his wife and his children, and will ostensibly offer loyalty in return. This has the effect of putting him at the top and putting the other family members in the position of reporting to him. In this situation, it will be difficult for bonding between the mother and children and between the siblings to occur, particularly when the narcissistic father is around.

On the other hand, if the father committed his sense of loyalty to the family, and if the other family members did the same, it would foster the growth of relationships and bonds between all family members. But the command and control system instituted by the narcissistic father ensures that he is always in control. In these situations, the wife and children dare not act without the express permission of their narcissistic controller. Thus his control of the actions of all the family members enables him to protect himself from them exposing his emotional state and making him face his ever-present underlying narcissistic feelings of self-loathing and low self-worth.

The narcissistic father depends on his family as an admiring audience to help validate his self-esteem. He displays bias towards those family members who give him positive feedback or admiration, which he yearns for, and he is disparaging towards those family members who fail to give him the positive feedback he craves. Over time, all family members learn to tell him what he wants to hear – it's the only way to avoid incurring his wrath.

In reality, the narcissistic father only understands the concept of loyalty in terms of others who are loyal to him – those who do his bidding and acknowledge his 'superiority'.

The Evolving Narcissist

'Personal relations founded on reflected glory, on the need to admire and be admired, prove fleeting and insubstantial.' [5]

Beware of telling a narcissist what or how you think. Divulging your innermost thoughts is possibly the worst thing you can do. You are, in effect, handing your self over to him. Every time you confide in him, his ability to control and manipulate your behaviour increases.

It's as though he's a virus that mutates. Every time you think you are back in control, you find that your antidote to his power becomes ineffective. The virus can take a long time to gain complete control over you, but gain complete control it will if you are exposed to it for long enough. If you are in any way codependent, by divulging your innermost thoughts to the narcissist, you will expose yourself to becoming completely infected by the virus, to the extent that you see the world in the same way that he does. You will become paranoid and envious, fearing and disliking the good people around you and sympathising with and defending the bad.

And then things get worse, for a narcissist is in many ways worse than a virus. A virus is unable to think, so although it makes you feel bad, eventually either your defences become sufficiently strong to fight it off, or you die. Where dealing with a narcissist is concerned, however, for some, the latter of these two outcomes would be preferable to succumbing to him.

The problem is that most, if not all, narcissists are intelligent – pathological, but intelligent. Once he has destroyed your defences, such that you now see the world as he does – that is, as threatening – he goes on to transform himself into a parasite. He can then continue to milk you in order to feed his needs, including his ego's needs, until you are of no use to him, or until he gets a better offer.

Even at this stage you are in a 'lose-lose' situation. If you have nothing to offer him you may be such a wreck that you may never recover, at least not to anywhere near your former self. But if you still have something to offer, he'll keep you hanging on and take what you have.

Your sole purpose since meeting and placing your trust in the narcissist has been to feed his ego, acting as a life-support mechanism for him, to the extent that you keep the virus and the parasite alive and you yourself end up needing help to survive, your dreams and aspirations destroyed.

What happened to that charming person you used to fight and beat, who would go out of his way to help you, your friends and your family? He was always there when you wanted him, considerate and protective, that lovable rogue. Everybody liked him, so he can't possibly be bad – can he? You know that you are intelligent, and you consider yourself to be a reasonably good judge of character, so it is highly unlikely that you have misjudged him – isn't it?

The answer is that you haven't misjudged him, you have misjudged yourself. It is your egotism that allows him to manipulate you, and therefore your behaviour. Your behaviour is narcissistic to some degree, not pathological like his, but it is narcissistic nonetheless.

In fact, you need to be codependent to some degree in order for there to be a mutual attraction between you and the narcissist. But in every codependent there is a narcissist trying to get out. Your narcissist friend allows your narcissism to emerge – in fact, he encourages it, knowing that he will always be in control. Codependents can never beat narcissists in battles of the ego. You become a victim, but you don't know it.

To become a victim there needs to be an element of narcissistic behaviour on your part at the beginning of your relationship, when the narcissist reflects you back to yourself; this is why he appears so charming. He allows you to love your own reflection. Some examples of the ego massaging that the narcissist indulges in are when he says: 'You look great in that'; 'You are perfect'; 'Is there anything you're not good at?' and so on. He says all the things that you wanted your parents to say to you when you were young. In this way he endears himself to you, and you will never want to believe the truth – that he is actually indifferent towards you. But the truth is that he only pretends to admire you so that you will admire him in return.

But you now feel good about yourself. From feeling unloved or downtrodden, you now feel in control. It's a nice feeling, and you associate it with your new narcissistic companion.

However, it doesn't last. Despite him working incessantly to impress you, your friends and your family so that everyone admires him and gives him the ego boosts he constantly craves, his indifference towards you means that if he encounters a better source of admiration and adulation, he will lack the moral and ethical character to reject it.

Connor was brought up by a single mother. He was honest, hard working, trusting in character and a competent manager, and he got on well with his boss, Nacer, who promoted him to the position of manager in order to work directly over him. But Nacer was highly narcissistic and really wanted Connor to work with him for two reasons: to do most of his work for him, and to be an additional source of admiration to feed his ego.

Connor did not seem to have typical codependency traits, although he did often act to protect Nacer from the consequences of his behaviour. He treated Nacer as someone to turn to when he needed something – advice, for example, which Nacer was always keen to offer. In reality, Connor's behaviour towards Nacer displayed paternal transference characteristics – he appeared to view Nacer as a substitute father figure. Connor appeared to respect Nacer's views, even if he didn't take on his world view in its entirety; this appeared to be sufficient for Nacer to feel that he had an admirer, and so a suitable source to engineer boosts to his ego when required.

Although Connor did not take on Nacer's world view in its entirety, he did tend to follow his advice, and followed examples set by Nacer's behaviour. Connor eschewed opportunities to advance himself through management training, and started smoking, like his substitute father figure.

Connor was happily married with children, but it was possible to identify symptoms of the anxiety and stress he was feeling at work as a result of his close association with a narcissist. He took time off sick because of feeling too much stress, and when asked why he had taken up smoking at work, he said that it helped numb the mental pain he felt.

A revealing symptom of difficulty he felt in his managerial position was when he spoke of a recurring dream he was having. It involved him driving over a bridge that went over the sea, but he never reached the end of the bridge, and he felt frustrated that no matter how fast he drove, or how long he drove for, the end of the bridge never came into view. Whilst dreams are always open to different interpretations, it is difficult not to relate this one to Connor's position in his working environment.

One of the reasons Nacer promoted Connor to that position was for him to do Nacer's job for him. This enabled Nacer to come and go as he pleased, knowing that he had a competent manager to deal with everything, cover up for him when necessary, and feed back to him everything that he needed to know. In effect, there were two people being paid to do one job. Nacer could take the credit as the senior manager, yet didn't have the responsibility of getting the work done, and he had someone to blame if anything went wrong – typical narcissistic behaviour. But this left Connor in a difficult position. He had no prospects of promotion, no prospects of gaining higher qualifications to move him forward, no prospects of doing anything other than acting as a prop to maintain his boss, and to protect him from the consequences of his behaviour when required. As a young, competent and ambitious manager with a family to support, Connor was working hard to get somewhere in life, but, like the end of the bridge in his dream, that somewhere was never going to come into view whilst he was working for a narcissist.

Connor, being honest, made the mistake of trusting and confiding in a narcissist, Nacer. He was happy to divulging his innermost thoughts, thus leaving himself at the mercy of Nacer, who used this knowledge to control and manipulate Connor's life. Connor felt ill at ease with himself, anxious and stressed, and developed coping mechanisms to get by, such as smoking and taking time off, away from his narcissistic boss. But he was still not able to make the connection between his anxiety and stress, and his reliance on a boss who pretended to have his interests at heart, but who in truth was indifferent towards him.

9

Morals and Ethics

How Should We Deal with Narcissistic Behaviour?

Philosophy can help you understand how best to live your life, and how others live theirs.

Narcissists are not interested enough in others to try to understand them, or even to care about meeting their needs. They learn just enough to enable them to manipulate others to meet their own needs. This behaviour is neither just nor honourable; it's neither moral nor ethical. So how should we deal with it?

Once you realise that you are being used, that your narcissistic spouse, work colleague, partner, friend, father, mother is only there for you to help meet his or her personal needs, such as status, security, sex, financial support or social opportunities, should you confront them and try to change them? Perhaps you should accept the way they are; after all, they can't help it. As Kant said, 'The world we perceive is constituted by the mind', and the world the narcissist perceives is an unfriendly, threatening place. He feels an over-whelming need to defend himself at all times.

Whether to try and change them is a tricky question. Narcissists have a right to live on this earth the same as everyone else, even though their moral and ethical behaviour may not coincide with the majority view of the world. But in order for them to survive, they make others suffer. It may not be that they want others to suffer; it may be that the part of their brain that deals with sympathy and compassion has not developed, so they are unable to empathise with others. Is this their fault, or is it the fault of their parents, who perhaps brought them up in an environment that nurtured their narcissistic tendencies? Should we blame their parents, or their parents' parents? Should we blame anyone? As their victims, we could of course blame ourselves for allowing ourselves to be snared – after all, other people can inflict physical pain on us against our will, but very rarely can they make our minds suffer without our tacit consent.

So how do we deal with a narcissist? Can he be beaten? Should we even try to beat him? None of these questions can be answered with a simple yes or no. If we try and beat the narcissist, we are then playing his game; and to him it's all about winning. It is not usually wise to take on someone who is an expert in his field, and a narcissist is undoubtedly an expert in the field of narcissism.

Professor Lou Marinoff, a philosophical counsellor, described how a client of his, Ed, had very noisy neighbours.[1] The occupants of the apartment above Ed didn't appear to be able to walk without stomping or to talk without shouting all hours of the day and night. Also, they had a seemingly endless stream of guests, and blasted out the stereo and television continuously. Unfortunately for Ed, he worked from home.

Professor Marinoff identified six courses of action for Ed. He could try and block out the noise by soundproofing, listening to his own music or watching television through headphones. He tried, but the noise penetrated his defences.

The second course involved being neighbourly, sitting down with them and making them aware of the problems they were causing him, and seeing if they were prepared to cooperate by finding ways of reducing the disturbance. This, of course, didn't work either. The bad neighbours were clearly lacking in empathy.

From a moral and ethical point of view, Professor Marinoff and Ed agreed that although the neighbours' parents had had a duty to their children which included allowing them sufficient play time and social time, they had also had a duty to teach their children to be considerate to others, including their neighbours. So, having tried the defensive and neighbourly options, Ed concluded that it was fair and reasonable for him to go on the offensive. He filed a complaint against his neighbours, and they were fined for disturbing his peace. But it still didn't work. In fact, the neighbours got worse.

Next Ed considered fighting fire with fire – making lots of noise himself to give them a taste of their own medicine. But he refrained from doing this on the basis of his belief that two wrongs don't make a right.

Ed then considered avoiding the situation by trying not to be home during the periods he knew would be the worst in terms of disturbance to him. But this was a non-starter as he worked from home.

Finally, Ed found the solution: he moved out to a quieter place. He recognised that part of the problem was his own intolerance of noise.

Ed was faced with the problem that many others, including codependents, are faced with when stuck in the same environment as narcissists. There are potentially lots of options available, but finding the right one is difficult. Some might view the option that Ed took as losing the battle, being beaten. But this presupposes that there was a battle in the first place.

When dealing with a narcissist, it is the narcissist who lays down the challenge. He wants to be in control. It is part of his makeup to feel that he must either be in control or have the perception of being in control, and he will never give up until he achieves this. But it only becomes a battle if you respond to the challenge that the narcissist has laid down. We don't know if Ed's noisy neighbours had grown up with a narcissistic parent, although I would think this was very likely, but the principle remains the same: it is highly unlikely that you will change a narcissist, so the next best option is to change your environment.

You may wonder why Harvey in Chapter 7 didn't adopt a similar strategy to Ed. Why didn't he change his environment when faced with a narcissist showing what appeared to be acute paranoia and pathological envy? He could have moved on, but he didn't. Like Ed, he had to make a choice about how best to live his life.

Have you ever wondered how best to do this, and how to find true happiness? You may not yet have found the answer. But why try to reinvent the wheel? Some philosophers over the last two and a half thousand years have applied a great deal of careful and systematic thinking to understanding how best to live your life. It's not as if these thinkers were not aware of narcissism; it was, after all, over two thousand years ago that the Greeks wrote about the first narcissist, a vain youth named Narcissus who was indifferent to Echo, a beautiful girl who fell in love with him.

Echo was in love with the handsome young Greek, Narcissus, but he was only in love with his own reflection. Narcissus watched his reflection in a pool until he died of starvation. Echo was in love with Narcissus, but could not express her love as she could only repeat the last syllables of what someone had said.

The story of Narcissus and Echo symbolises the tragedy of missed opportunities, because they both had mistaken views of love. Narcissus loved simply a reflection; Echo loved someone who could not love another. The Greek myth thus explores a sad situation that left both the narcissistic Narcissus and the codependent Echo unhappy and unfulfilled.

How best to live your life, or how to relieve suffering of the mind, is a recurring theme in the works of many of the great philosophers; including Socrates, Plato, Aristotle, Kierkegaard and Mill. Whilst their analyses vary, there are some common threads that run through all of their thoughts and deliberations.

Philosophy is defined by some as 'love of wisdom'. It uses reason and argument to gain knowledge of the world we live in. Knowledge can be acquired in many ways, including through education. As Aristotle said, 'Education is the best provision for the journey to old age.' As we use doctors to solve physical problems, so we should use philosophers when our soul is unwell.[2] 'Just as medicine confers no benefit if it does not drive away physical illness, so philosophy is useless if it does not drive away the suffering of the mind.'[3]

The latter part of Socrates' life was taken up by him trying to impart his ethical views to the citizens of Athens. Kirkegaard considered how it was possible to live an ethical life, but concluded that the purely ethical life was a non-starter. There is more to life than pure ethical behaviour – though life without an ethical dimension is also not possible. Kirkegaard considered that life must also consist of aesthetic, maybe even hedonistic, and religious elements.

Plato himself reached a similar conclusion. Although rather puritan in his approach to the aesthetic side of human behaviour, he believed that life should be lived ethically; and he also believed in the existence of god(s). He described how he analysed the different elements of the human mind and concluded that its well-being, full development and happiness are achieved by behaving ethically.

Epicurus was said to have lived a promiscuous or hedonistic lifestyle to the full, before realising the error of his ways. In fact, he lent his name to the 'epicurean' lifestyle. However, he eventually realised that it was not possible to achieve enduring happiness without living a virtuous, ethical lifestyle.

On the other hand, there were some philosophers who, despite having brilliant intellects, found that happiness was anathema. Schopenhauer, Heidegger, Nietzsche and Machiavelli all wrote little about the achievement of happiness; but maybe it was because each had their own good reasons for doing so. Schopenhauer was perhaps the greatest pessimist in the history of philosophy; Heidegger lived in Germany during the Nazi era, although he appeared to embrace Nazism at the outset; Nietzsche was plagued by illness until he died insane; and Machiavelli seemed to think that ethical behaviour didn't bring much benefit.

Machiavelli appeared to believe more in unscrupulous, ruthless cunning than in honesty and integrity. However, his interests were in the world of political leadership, and he argued that excessively merciful leadership would do more harm to a community through disorder than cruel leadership that maintains order through fear. He may well have been right in the world he lived in, but it is still possible to be a leader with strength, fortitude and the ability to act quickly and decisively, and at the same time behave ethically. Take Mahatma Gandhi in India or Nelson Mandela in South Africa, for example.

The great philosophers not only guide us towards answering the question of how to live a morally and ethically good life, but also teach us a great deal more in understanding the nature of reality and other issues necessary to understand the world in which we live.

The view of Socrates was that the goal of philosophy is to seek truth and to live justly. Some two and a half thousand years later, the contemporary philosopher Anthony O'Hear stated concisely the only way real enduring happiness can be achieved: 'There cannot be true self-esteem without self-worth, and self-worth has to be earned. Nor is there real happiness outside of a life well lived, of which happiness is the by-product.'[4]

Boosts to your self-esteem achieved by self-aggrandisement, the denigration of others, shopping, alcohol or drugs are only transient. Trying to insulate yourself from life's challenges through filling your time with distractions such as junk television programmes or drinking alcohol to excess will only serve to lower your self-esteem further over time. This behaviour, using 'quick fixes' to boost your ego, is described by Kierkegaard as 'aesthetic'.

In contrast, being honest with yourself and others, facing up to the challenges of life – both physical and emotional – and overcoming them builds character, self-belief, self-esteem and self-worth; with which comes the much sought-after side effect of happiness. This behaviour is described by Kierkegaard as ethical. And an ethical person is still capable of aesthetic enjoyment. As Aristotle said, 'I count him braver who overcomes his desires than him who conquers his enemies; for the hardest victory is over self.'

So where does this leave the narcissist? Is he happy? The narcissist is the antithesis of a truly happy person, if most of the great philosophers over the last two and a half thousand years are to be believed. Narcissists continually attempt to boost their self-esteem by self-aggrandisement and the disparagement of others; they also tend to indulge in 'transient' activities such as drug-taking, gambling, shopping, alcohol and extra-marital sex. So, typically, they indulge in immoral and unethical behaviour. This suggests an unhappy person who continually seeks short-term pleasure through a variety of distractions to avoid feelings of low self-esteem and low self-worth.

But if you ask a narcissist whether he is happy, he will always answer 'yes'. On the other hand, we know that he has no compunction whatsoever about lying to protect himself from a perceived ego threat. Perhaps he doesn't know any different; he believes that the only way to live his life is to trust no one. Although he looks after his codependent and mutually dependent 'friends', because mistreating them may well result in a painful response, he still doesn't trust them – he just uses them.

And we have the same problem with codependents as we do with narcissists. We know that they trust no one and tell lies to protect themselves from emotional threats, as well as to protect their narcissist. So are they happy? Perhaps they are, but only when in the company of their narcissistic controller.

Happiness may be relative. O'Hear's belief that there is no real happiness outside of a life well lived, of which happiness is the by-product, may be confirmed by those who have had a life 'well lived' and therefore have the knowledge to say whether it is true. But if you have not had a life 'well lived', how can you compare your level of happiness with someone who has had a life 'well lived'?

Children who have grown into narcissists or codependents have typically been brought up in a dysfunctional family environment where a narcissistic parent, typically the father, has suppressed their free expression of thought. Gordon was such a father. He controlled his children over many years by repeatedly shouting at them, 'You're useless', 'You're stupid' and 'You're a waste of space'. You may wonder why the children's mother never came to the aid of her children. Perhaps she didn't because of the control he also appears to have exhibited over her. For example, on one occasion, from his front drive he shouted at her for all to hear, 'You f***ing slag'; she slammed the front door shut and he then drove off down the road as though he was competing in a dragster race.

Children are emotionally vulnerable. As Professor Marinoff stated, 'To call a child stupid once is offensive; to repeat that on a daily basis is harmful.'[5] Children exposed to the behaviour exhibited by Gordon are, in effect, being groomed to become either narcissistic or codependent. We established earlier in the Stanford University prison study that narcissists and codependents are just opposite sides of the same coin, so to speak; which side they end up as depends on their environment. Gordon's behaviour, and the complementary behaviour of his wife, provide the ideal preparation for the next generation of narcissists and codependents. Their children are likely to grow up into narcissists and/or codependents, thereby perpetuating the problem. If a child grows up in a family environment where free expression of thought has been suppressed by a parent and he graduates from there to a family of his own where he is the parent, he will then be the one who suppresses free expression of thought. It is how he has been brought up, so it follows that he will believe that this environment is normal; he or she does not know any other. The immoral and unethical behaviour of the father has been passed on to his offspring. So the child who later becomes the parent in this situation may never know what true happiness is. He has never experienced it. He has never had a life 'well lived'. This suggests that the narcissist who says he is happy may well be telling the truth; happiness is relative. In fact, he may actually be happier as a parent than he was as a child, as he is now the one in control, as opposed to being the one being controlled.

So how important is moral and ethical behaviour to our happiness? Perhaps we need to look again at some of the great thinkers of the western world over the last two and a half thousand years to answer this question.

Is Moral and Ethical Behaviour Important?

The pleasures of the aesthetic are short-lived and unreliable, while the pleasures of the ethical are compassionate and long-lasting.

Many people believe that there is a lack of clear moral thinking in society today. Aristotle's *Ethics* was written in the fourth century BC, but since then human beings seem to have progressed painfully slowly with regard to extending the application of ethical behaviour widely in our society.

Aristotle said 'a complete life' is required for happiness. The young are neither happy nor unhappy. We can only judge whether we have had a happy life when we reach the end of it. So it follows that how we behave on the way is crucial to our happiness.

If a man spends his life denying his wrongdoing by telling lies, distorting the truth and generally behaving unethically, as narcissists typically do, as he ages and looks back on his life, will he be proud of his achievements? Will doing so bring him pride and pleasure? Will it make him happy? But at what point does unethical behaviour make him unhappy? Is it a gradual process? Or can he continue denying his wrongdoing until the very end of his life?

The problem is that at some point, sooner or later, if he is in any way religious he will have to start thinking about going to heaven or going to hell when he dies. If he's not religious, he won't be able to avoid thinking about his life on earth, what he has been, what he is. And what he is can only be determined by the sum of his activities so far, his deeds, and his actions, good and bad. The narcissist will most likely deny that any decision has to be made, consciously; but we all have an unconscious, the storage area of the brain that feeds information back into the conscious without us realising where it has come from. Will his unconscious be trying to make the decision about whether he is going to heaven or hell; if it does, will this cause anxiety and pain?

In *Either/Or*,[6] Kierkegaard identified two central types of existence, the aesthetic and the ethical; he also recognised a religious

117

existence. The aesthetic referred to personal, sensory experiences and involved living for the moment. It involves a pleasure-seeking, largely materialistic and hedonistic lifestyle, although it finds its highest expression in music, the theatre, and love. The ethical involved an obligation to living a social and morally proper life, fulfilling obligations, being honest with oneself and others. The religious life involved accepting the ethical ideals as part of a wider obligation to humanity and God.

The pleasures of the aesthetic are short-lived and unreliable, while the pleasures of the ethical are compassionate and long-lasting. But Kierkegaard believed that dissatisfaction with the aesthetic and ethical elements of life was the cause of feelings of guilt and anxiety. The alternative was a religious existence.

Kierkegaard didn't advocate a purely ethical or religious lifestyle; he recognised that human beings make choices motivated by both aesthetic and ethical reasons, that there is a human need for pleasure seeking. However, he did believe that humans can only be sure of doing the right thing by trying to do God's will. Only by accepting that God is always right and by trying to do God's will can a person escape unhappiness.

On the other hand, Albert Einstein didn't believe that an ethical lifestyle should be linked to doing God's will. In a letter to Max Born on 4 December 1926, he wrote:

A man's ethical behaviour should be based effectually on sympathy, education, and social ties; no religious basis is necessary. Man would indeed be in a poor way if he had to be restrained by fear of punishment and hope of reward after death.

Einstein was not a philosopher, he was a scientist, albeit a brilliant scientist; but perhaps he had a point.

The point is, though, that it doesn't really matter whether God exists or not. It is the belief that you are doing the right thing, being honest, kind, and thoughtful to others, that matters. We need a direction to point towards. If pointing towards God enables you to behave in a moral and ethical way, and as a consequence it brings you happiness, you don't need to prove God's existence; belief is enough.

Many of the greatest thinkers of the last twenty-five centuries, including Socrates, Plato, Aristotle, Kierkegaard, Epicurus and Mill, suggest that leading an ethical life will at least lay the foundation to relieve suffering of the mind.

Are Narcissists Conscious of their Behaviour?

'Watch your thoughts; they become words.
Watch your words; they become actions.
Watch your actions; they become habits.
Watch your habits; they become character.
Watch your character; it becomes your destiny.'[7]

It is easy to dismiss the thought that our unconscious makes the decisions that cause us pain and anxiety, for aren't all our decisions made consciously? It will come as a surprise to many people that there is substantive evidence that our unconscious mind makes our decisions for us, before we are conscious of them.

In a famous series of experiments, Dr Benjamin Libet demonstrated that brain activity initiating a movement, of say the hand, precedes awareness of the movement, thus suggesting that consciousness is not causal. If this is so, free will is a delusion.[8]

Dr Libet measured the response time between the moment the brain of a patient was stimulated and the time the patient became consciously aware of the stimulus. He found there was a consistent half-second delay between the unconscious reaction and conscious awareness of the stimulus.

He continued his work with more experiments involving the use of electrodes to measure the response times of the brain. He found, for example, that when a volunteer was instructed to move a finger, the brain unconsciously initiated the movement even before the volunteer was aware that the finger had begun moving.

Dr Libet pointed out that his experiments did not indicate that 'free will' did not exist in humans at all, because if his subjects were told not to move a finger, or to stop moving it, their conscious would maintain complete control. He explained that in respect of the unconscious movement of the finger they could 'veto it and block performance of the act'.

Susan Pockett summarised Libet's work as follows:

> These conclusions are important to consciousness researchers precisely because they seem to deny to consciousness any major role in our day-to-day affairs. If we cannot become conscious of external stimuli until half a second after they happen, then even mildly fast reaction to a stimulus has to be unconsciously generated. Worse, not only are reactions necessarily unconscious, but even proactive or 'voluntary' actions must be unconsciously generated. So if consciousness is important at all, it can only be in the generation of long-term plans, which are then carried out unconsciously.[9]

It appears that consciousness does not contribute to the initiation of thoughts or actions, but it does retain a role in overruling thoughts or actions instigated by the unconscious.

So if our unconscious is at the root of all our decisions – not just the big ones, but those innumerable decisions we make on a minute-by-minute or even second-by-second basis during our waking hours – it must eventually be converted into our actions. Our behaviour is determined by our unconscious. And if our unconscious is formed by our underlying attitude to morals and ethics, it follows that our morals and ethics determine our behaviour.

Thus, whilst the narcissist can control his conscious thought, he cannot control his unconscious thought. His behaviour is initially controlled by his unconscious thought, those negative emotional thoughts deposited there during his formative early years. They constantly bombard his psyche, supplying a continuous stream of triggers which keep him on high alert looking for threats to his ego. But he is able to moderate his behaviour through his conscious thought. He develops high-speed thought processes as he deals with the stream of triggers from his unconscious, and moderates their demands to ensure that he is able to project his well-practised false image. This process enables him to constantly engineer the positive feedback that he needs to maintain equilibrium.

As a consequence, the ageing narcissist, having led a life denying his wrongdoing by telling lies and distorting the truth and generally behaving immorally and unethically, may look back on it with some regret, anxiety and pain. As Buddha said, 'As you think, so shall you become.'

10

Happiness

How is Happiness Achieved?

The happiness of your life depends on the quality of your thoughts.[1]

André Comte-Sponville wrote: 'Happiness is probably no more than loving who you are, what you have and what you do.'[2] If he is right, we all have within us the ability to achieve happiness. But how do we get there? Is it through careful planning, or is it through luck? Many believe that whether you are happy or not is just the luck of the draw, particularly those who are not happy. There may be some truth in it. You can't choose your parents, and it is usually your parents through their genes and the environment they (or your carers) provide for you that determine how you develop. But if you are not happy, perhaps through anxiety and/or depression, there is much you can do to change things.

But there are no short cuts to achieving happiness. The quick fixes – shopping, alcohol, drugs and so on – only give temporary respite before another quick fix is required. This aesthetic behaviour works, but it only papers over the cracks. A longer-term solution is required to prevent the problems resurfacing, again and again and again.

Love brings happiness, and it's widely recognised that you need to love yourself before you can love others. It is often said that narcissists love themselves, but if they do, it's a pathological love that manifests itself through behaviour that is habitual, maladaptive and compulsive.

'Philosophy' comes from the Greek word *philosophia*, meaning love of wisdom; and wisdom is 'happiness without illusion or lies'. So can philosophy make us happy? Epicurus, another Greek philosopher, believed that it can; he wrote: 'Philosophy is an activity, which, through discourse and reasoning, procures for us a happy life.'[3]

The answer to the question of whether philosophy can make us happy is, therefore, a qualified yes. The qualification is that philosophy per se can't make us happy, but through discourse and reasoning we can gain wisdom and think better, and by thinking better we can live better. And as Anthony O'Hear wrote, 'the only way real enduring happiness can be achieved is through a life well lived, of which happiness is the by-product'.[4]

To gain wisdom, we need to get rid of any illusions or lies. Some people, narcissists for example, lie and distort the truth to create a false image of themselves and others – an illusion. Codependents take on their narcissist's view of the world and promulgate the lies and distortions. Being honest with yourself, not using denial and distortion of facts as a defence against feeling bad about yourself, is difficult but worthwhile in the quest for happiness.

So, why are narcissists important in a discussion about achieving happiness in one's life? The answer lies in their behaviour, which can seriously diminish the happiness of those around them, including that of their codependent associates. They continually create stressful situations for themselves and others, which, over time, creates anxiety and depression – for others, not necessarily for themselves.

Narcissists think of themselves as being at the centre of the universe; everyone must recognise this fact and behave accordingly. This is probably because when they were young they were spoiled, and they expect this pattern to continue. Only spoilt children develop the notion that they can demand. Narcissists are people with low self-esteem who attempt to control others' views of them for defensive purposes. Their success depends on receiving support from a codependent support network, usually either family members or colleagues at work, and they are ruthless when it comes to obtaining resources – including emotional, physical and material resources.

Narcissists need people around them to supply these resources, including, most importantly, emotional resources. To achieve this, they maintain a balance between over-controlling and under-controlling their codependent partners. This is where the highs and lows of a relationship with a narcissist have their root, and if you are codependent, this is also where your anxiety and periods of depression may come from. To be happy you need to be in control; but you never are if you always have to feed the emotional, physical and material needs of a narcissist.

Ultimately, narcissists may become anxious and depressed themselves, particularly if they lose their codependent support network. A life of lies, distortion, denial, paranoia and envy will inevitably take its toll.

But remember, if you are the victim of a narcissist you may not be entirely innocent yourself. As we established in Chapter 8, to become a victim there needs to be an element of narcissistic behaviour on your part at the beginning of your relationship when the narcissist reflects you back to yourself; this is why he appears so charming. He allows you to love your own reflection.

Dr Alan Rappoport uses the term 'co-narcissist' to describe people who 'work hard to please others, defer to others' opinions, worry about how others think and feel about them, are often depressed or anxious, find it hard to know their own views and experience, and take the blame for interpersonal problems. They fear being considered selfish if they act assertively.'[5] They are like this because of their attempts to get along with their narcissistic parents during childhood. Co-narcissists, or codependents, have been primed by their parent(s) to become a narcissist's prey. And as Dr Rappoport states, a high proportion of psychotherapy patients are codependent, suffering from anxiety and/or depression.

The codependent is the mirror image of the narcissist. In a relationship between two codependents, one will adopt the narcissist's dominant position. The codependent has been brought up to believe that in any interpersonal interaction, one person is narcissistic and the other codependent. So one codependent adopts the role of the narcissist, whilst the other continues as a codependent, and takes the blame for interpersonal problems.

Unfortunately for the narcissists' codependent victims, and for the codependents who adopt the role of the narcissist, eventually they realise that their lives are either being controlled or are out of control. They don't have healthy means of self-expression. As we have already established, a prerequisite to happiness is being in control, or at least having the perception of being in control, without which anxiety and/or depression results.

It is widely recognised that changing a malignant narcissist for the better is all but impossible. But there is hope for codependents, although it can be extremely difficult to wean her from her narcissist. The codependent feels obliged to protect the narcissist. Any suggestion that her behaviour is in any way dysfunctional, or that her relationship with her narcissist is dysfunctional, will be met with robust denial. The codependent will protect her narcissist at all costs.

To achieve happiness, the need to be honest with yourself is paramount. Denial − failure to acknowledge what is going on − is the first obstacle that must be overcome. However, this becomes almost impossible for a codependent who continues to interact with his or her narcissist. The codependent unconsciously assumes that everyone else is narcissistic also, so finds it extremely difficult to develop a relationship in which neither individual dominates. But this is what is required − a relationship in which neither person has a need to dominate the other, and in which each can appreciate what the other has to offer.

It may be difficult for a codependent to enter into such a relationship without creating tension through reacting to, or provoking, their partner. For example, if the partner doesn't adopt a dominant role in the relationship, as a narcissist would, the codependent will feel the need to adopt the role instead. It may then be necessary for the codependent to consult a therapist/counsellor.

By getting on with life without the influence of a narcissistic controller, the codependent may, with or without help, develop an understanding of how non-narcissistic relationships work, and by adopting a moral and ethical view of life it may well be possible to eradicate most of the feelings of anxiety and depression and lay the foundations for happiness.

How Do You Know You Have Achieved True Happiness and Not Just Transitory Pleasure?

'We must not let ourselves believe that pure pleasure consists of relief from pain.'[6]

After beginning the process of ameliorating the feelings of anxiety and depression, the next step towards finding happiness needs to be identified, but Plato believed that the great majority of people would never be able to identify this step and experience true happiness. He described how people find pleasure in the relief of pain or anxiety, believing it to be happiness, but said that this pleasure is not true happiness, just an illusory belief that happiness had been found.

In his *Republic*, after describing in great detail his ideal society led by the 'philosopher king', Plato goes on to describe four imperfect types of society – timarchy, oligarchy, democracy, and tyranny – giving reasons why they might follow on from each other. For each society he identifies a corresponding individual – for example, 'democratic man' in a democracy, and 'tyrant' in a tyranny. The characteristics of these individuals are those, Plato states, which will be admired in the society to which they correspond. The characteristics of the tyrant correspond closely to those of the narcissist already described in this book; think of Joseph Stalin, Adolf Hitler or Saddam Hussein.

The timarchic society would have originated from Plato's ideal state, and the rulers can be described as military aristocracy. The oligarchic society is one which is controlled by wealthy individuals known as oligarchs, whose sole object is to make money. The democratic society appears when the friction between the ever-more-greedy rulers and the citizens comes to a head. Finally the democratic society gives way to tyranny, and Plato describes how the tyrant flourishes in a democratic society.

The demise of the democratic state is brought about by the conflict between rich and poor and the tyrant's rise as popular champion, bringing about the growth of oppression. Democracy inevitably leads to an excessive desire for liberty at the expense of everything else. Democratic demands will lead to the election of rulers who behave like their subjects, which means that the subjects will imitate their rulers.

Plato went on to explain what will happen at lower levels of society, describing with amazing accuracy what appears to be developing more and more in contemporary western society:

> The teacher fears and panders to his pupils, who in turn despise their teachers and attendants; and the young as a whole imitate their elders, argue with them and set themselves up against them, while their elders try to avoid the reputation of being disagreeable or strict by aping the young and mixing with them on terms of easy good fellowship.[7]

Plato depicts three groups in a democratic society. First, he illustrates a class of 'thriftless idlers' by comparing them with drones. The energetic leaders of these thriftless idlers he calls drones with stings, whereas the more inert mass of followers he calls drones without stings. The narcissistic tyrant equates to a drone with a sting, whilst the drones without stings can be likened to the narcissists' codependent followers. Plato said that whenever these two elements appear in society they cause trouble.

The second group that inevitably emerges from the masses is what Plato calls 'the steadiest characters', who are the most successful at making money. The third group is the largest – the mass of the people who take little interest in politics; they just want to work for a living without getting too involved.

Democratic society, therefore, deteriorates as moral and ethical values fall and those in the drone group extract money from the rich, keeping as much of the proceeds for themselves as they can, and distributing the rest to the masses to keep them quiet. This behaviour will ultimately undermine the democratic society, leading to the appointment of a single popular leader, from which tyranny invariably springs.

The decline in behaviour and moral values described by Plato in his explanation of how a democracy degenerates into a tyranny is symptomatic of today's society. Lack of respect for those in authority – pupils failing to respect their teachers, for example – is indicative of a society suffering from stress and anxiety. This view is supplemented by the large numbers of people seeking relief from their cerebral problems through the 'happy' drugs such as Prozac.

The circumstances that cause anxiety and despair are not usually biological abnormalities such as the often-quoted chemical imbalance to which many people rashly attribute their so-called stress or depression; they are, rather, environmental, caused by events in life, such as being brought up by one narcissistic and one codependent parent, leaving children and young adults ill-equipped to deal with the challenges of life.

The defence mechanism of denial, used extensively by narcissists and codependents alike, may ultimately result in them suffering both mentally and physically. Research by Margie Lachman and others[8] revealed that it is beneficial to have a realistic view of both the past and the future. People who accurately perceive their past and future happiness tend to suffer less depression and enjoy better health. Consequently, those narcissists and codependents who use denial to rewrite history in the way that they would have liked it to be, as opposed to perceiving their past the way it was, may be causing themselves psychological trauma through depression and also threatening their physical health.

Plato believed that the greater part of the most intense pleasure that we experience through our bodies are the feelings we get from the relief of pain, and that this is analogous to the natural world. He recounted a discussion between Socrates and Glaucon, Plato's younger half-brother:[9]

Socrates: Do you agree that in the natural world there is a top, a bottom, and a middle?

Glaucon: Yes.

S: Then won't anyone who rises from the bottom to the middle think that he has risen towards the top? And as he stands in the middle and looks down to where he came from, won't he think he's at the top, never having seen the real top?

G: I don't see how he could think anything else.

S: And suppose he then went down again, he would suppose he was going down to the bottom, and would be right.

G: Yes.

S: And would not all this happen to him because he had no experience of what top, middle, and bottom really were?

G: Obviously.

S: Then is it surprising that the views of men who lack experience of the truth should be unsound about pleasure and pain and the neutral state between them as they are about a good many other things? When they are subject to pain, they will think they are in pain and their pain will feel real. But they will be convinced that the transition from pain to the neutral state brings satisfaction and pleasure, whereas in fact their lack of experience of true pleasure leads them to make a false contrast between pain and the absence of pain.

The same can be said about a boy brought up by one narcissistic parent and one codependent parent, having his free expression of thought suppressed and being groomed to become either narcissistic or codependent in later adult life. If he graduates from a codependent boy to a narcissistic father, for example, he has, in Plato's terms, risen from the bottom to the middle. He may feel happy, relative to what has gone before, but he has never seen the top, true happiness.

Socrates later went on to summarise the conversation between himself and Glaucon:

> Those, therefore, who have no experience of wisdom and goodness, and do nothing but have a good time, spend their life straying between the bottom and the middle of our illustration, and never rise higher to see or reach the true top, nor achieve any real fulfilment or sure and unadulterated pleasure. They bend over their tables, like sheep with heads bent over their pasture and eyes on the ground, they stuff themselves and copulate, and in their greed for more they kick and butt each other ... because they are not satisfied, as they cannot be while they fill with unrealities a part of themselves which is itself unreal and insatiable.

Aristotle's belief that education is the best provision for the journey to old age is based on the fact that knowledge and wisdom remove fear and anxiety and its accompanying cerebral pain, allowing a person's natural state to rise from the bottom to the middle, and then onwards towards the top. Only when you have arrived at the top will you know that you have achieved true happiness. As Epictetus, the Greek Stoic philosopher who taught philosophy as a way of life and not just a theoretical discipline, said, 'Only the educated are free.'

Plato's belief that the great majority of people will never experience true happiness may well be true today. There are many who cannot find it. All they can do is search for relief of pain or anxiety, often through the use of alcohol or drugs, either legal or illegal, by way of a 'quick-fix' solution. But by taking a longer-term approach they could pass beyond the middle and achieve true happiness. Most people, however, could not realise this ideal without sustained support from people who understand the neurotic behaviour of narcissists and codependents alike.

Can Narcissists and Codependents Find Happiness?

'The summit of the human mountain is attained by finding one's identity as a unique human being, and not by losing it in self-transcending identification with groups.'[10]

The narcissist spends his time jockeying for position with other narcissists and with codependents. The positions are somewhere between the bottom and middle of Plato's natural world. When he reaches the middle, and all the other narcissists and codependents in his world are below him, the narcissist may think he has reached the summit and found true happiness.

Unfortunately, this state is very short lived as it is merely an illusion of happiness; so when he finds that he is still not happy he has to find another battle to win. In reality, he is only halfway up, unaware that there is a top above him. He's never experienced what people at the top feel – it is something out of his awareness. So the narcissist and his codependents, those people he has hooked and reeled in to help him in his futile pursuit of happiness, will spend their lives competing with others outside the group for what they perceive to be the top position. The narcissist will fight to achieve what he believes is happiness, the position where he can look down on those below: those narcissists of lesser strength than him, and those codependents who never stood a chance in the first place. But what about those people at the top, those 'normal' people who don't suffer mental distress? How does he perceive them? And how do codependents perceive them? These people at the top are those who get on with their lives; they are neither drones nor drones with a sting, so they don't pose a threat. They don't even try to claim the middle ground.

Both narcissists and codependents live in a dualistic world; they see every interpersonal relationship as one of leader–follower – one party must adopt the role of narcissistic leader, and one that of codependent follower. As stated earlier, the reason is most likely that they grew up with parents or carers who behaved in this way, and as a result, this harmful view of the world was implanted in them from an early age, so they (wrongly) believe that someone must take control in all interpersonal relationships.

> Plato explained how harmful ideas are sometimes implanted in us by others whom we trust, such as our parents, when we are young, vulnerable, and credulous. Although these ideas may later exert unwholesome constricting influences on us – like mental straightjackets – we may defend them nonetheless because we mistakenly believe they are our own.[11]

Consequently, relationships with those people who are on the normal spectrum are viewed by narcissists and codependents with distrust.

We can go back to what Manfred Kets de Vries stated as an approximation of the mental state of society today. He argues that 20 per cent of the general population are relatively healthy; 20 per cent are relatively sick; and the other 60 per cent, who all suffer from 'neurotic misery', are somewhere in the middle.[12] If we imagine a circle divided up like a pie chart with the 20 per cent of relatively healthy people at the top and the 20 per cent of relatively sick people at the bottom, we can divide the remaining 60 per cent suffering from 'neurotic misery' into two – thirty per cent on the left and thirty per cent on the right. The left thirty per cent represent the codependents, and the right thirty per cent represent the narcissists.

Both the codependents and the narcissists will be afflicted in varying degrees of 'neurotic misery', from those near the top who are predominantly healthy and those at the bottom who closely resemble those who are 'relatively sick' in the group beneath them. This mental picture gives as some idea of the extent of the problem across the general population, and is an approximate representation of western society today. If we discount the relatively sick at the bottom of the circle, most of whom are looked after one way or another, through hospitals, family carers, care homes for the elderly and so on, the remaining three segments serve the purpose of demonstrating the human trinity that influences so much of the behaviour in our civilisation.

At birth, a child is neither narcissistic nor codependent, but is dependent upon his or her genes and, to a larger extent, on the environmental influences during his or her upbringing; the philosopher John Locke believed that a child's mind at birth is like a blank slate waiting to be written on by the world of experience. Eventually the child will find or, perhaps more accurately, will be guided into his or her position on the circle.

Imagine that at birth the child is at the centre of the circle, and that during the period when he grows through childhood and adolescence into adulthood he travels from the centre outwards to the position on the circle perimeter that represents his emotional state when fully grown. He may be healthy, and therefore at or near the top, narcissistic, so on the right, codependent, so on the left, or disturbed and at or near the bottom; it depends upon his genes and life's influences along the way.

In early childhood, an infant who is subjected to an emotionally troubled parent will find that his first steps towards developing his emotional state will have been taken in entirely the wrong direction, particularly if that parent is the mother. The longer the child heads in the wrong direction, the less likely he will be able to find the right path and develop a healthy emotional state in adulthood.

Alice Miller described the case of Beatrice as an example of the emotional damage that a mother can do to a very young child. Beatrice was not physically mistreated in her youth, but she did have to learn as a small infant how to make her mother happy 'by not crying, by not being hungry – by not having any needs at all'. Beatrice suffered first from anorexia and then, throughout her adult life, from severe depression.[13]

Empirical research published in 2009 by Amanda Brandone and

Henry Wellman tended to confirm what Alice Miller had observed and written about thirty years earlier. It revealed that babies as young as ten months old had a surprisingly sophisticated understanding of other people's minds.[14]

Those who grow into normal adults without psychological hang-ups will have been parented in a way that promoted neither code-pendent nor narcissistic symptoms. They will have received unconditional love but with adequate discipline and the setting of boundaries, which will result in the child growing into an adult with a realistic self-image.

It doesn't mean to say that during their lifetime the normal adults will not encounter environmental conditions that cause them to stray into either codependent or narcissistic territory, but when this happens they will recognise that they are in an unfamiliar situation and that they are exhibiting uncharacteristic behaviour, and over time they will work towards returning to their natural position on the circle, in the normal region. We saw in Chapter 1, in Philip Zim-bardo's Stanford University prison study, how quickly the students reverted to uncharacteristic behaviour reminiscent of pathological narcissism in some cases, but once taken out of the artificial environment they quickly went back to their old ways.

However, prolonged exposure to a toxic environment, such as one where a narcissist whose view of the world is supported by his codependent supporters has gained control, will be challenging even to the most normal of people. As a result, it is possible that a normal person will change his perception of others to be more in line with that of the narcissist. We saw in Chapter 5 how narcissists distort the perceptions of the people around them so that over time they start to reflect the narcissist's view.

We discovered earlier how narcissists' success depends on them receiving support from a codependent support network. They cea-selessly work towards setting up a support network around them to supply the emotional, physical and material resources that they need. It may consist of their family group, their subordinates at work, or a social grouping. But most importantly, they must have this support network in place before they feel sufficiently confident to move from a defensive 'fear' position to a position of being proactive and aggressive.

Historically, groups have worked to the advantage of humans and helped support their survival in the face of threats from predators, but paradoxically, groups have always been the major source of conflict in human activities. Battles have been waged throughout history between groups, and have ranged in size from small family feuds to huge religious conflicts or national and international wars such as the world wars of the last century.

The root cause of these conflicts can usually be traced back to one narcissistic individual who has succeeded in gaining sufficient support to enable his pathological mind to exert its will over others. What is most unpalatable to the majority of people is the fact that the narcissistic individual always seems to be able to get others to carry out his frequently reprehensible deeds. Adolf Hitler is one of many such tyrants over the centuries who have caused incalculable damage to human beings, and yet who were able to distance themselves from the mayhem they caused whilst their narcissistic and codependent subordinates did the dirty work, the subordinates' perceptions having been distorted by the tyrants over time such that eventually they reflected the latters' view of the world.

It is, mercifully, very rare for narcissists to be as 'successful' as Hitler, but the impact of narcissistic leaders on groups as diverse as families, religious factions, businesses and government departments can be devastating for those who are not favoured by their pathological leader.

Through their inbuilt paranoia and envy, narcissistic leaders foster the view that their group is central to the cause and that it is an 'us' and 'them' situation. And always the 'us' is considered superior to the 'them'. Codependent members of the group can impress their narcissistic leader by disparaging his enemies at every available opportunity. If the process reaches the stage where group members are willing to dehumanise the members of the other group, then things can get out of hand. Hitler's dehumanisation of Jews is an extreme example of taking an 'us' and 'them' situation too far.

If being a member of a group led by a narcissist can have such profound consequences, why would anyone become a member? There are several answers to this question.

First, a person may join a group because of the benefits he or she derives from membership. A codependent person's emotional state is similar in many ways to that of the narcissist. Such people feel fear based on paranoia, with strong feelings of vulnerability when faced with even mildly threatening interpersonal relationships. Codependents tend to adopt submissive behaviour in these situations, as opposed to the narcissist, who would typically adopt an aggressive stance. As we identified in Chapter 2, codependents crave security so are attracted to narcissists, and as narcissists crave power, it is a natural symbiotic relationship. The codependent joins the group headed by the narcissist and, as part of the deal, the narcissist gives him protection when intimidating interpersonal relationships threaten. Whilst both the narcissist and the codependent know the reason why they have teamed up, both of them tacitly 'agree' not to discuss it to avoid any negative feelings.

These groups are found everywhere in present-day western society. They can be in family, social or work settings. The evidence is available from multiple sources. Look around you; speak to your family and friends. Observe the behaviour of others for the telltale signs. Look at the forums on the Internet such as the Psychopath and Narcissist Survivors Support Group, or look in your phone book for the domestic violence hotline in your area.

There are countless women in relationships with narcissistic boyfriends or husbands who were drawn into their relationship on this basis. Whilst many of these relationships endure and many of the women claim to be happy, there are many others where the female partner feels trapped. She is completely under the control of her narcissistic tormentor, but the option of leaving him is not available, as her codependency means that the perceived threat to her from the unknown is too dangerous. It is uncharted territory and she perceives the risks as too great for her to take the plunge and walk out.

It is not always the male who is the narcissist, of course. There are many women who adopt the controlling role in a relationship, and there are many codependent men, but these are in a minority. And it also applies to same sex relationships where a narcissist may exert complete control over a codependent partner.

Second, in line with the 'us' and 'them' relationships fostered by narcissistic leaders, it may be a case of either joining the group or running the risk of being excluded from everything. George was a manager who stood up to narcissistic posturing by his boss, a director called Peter. George was criticised for telling the truth and trying to establish an honest dialogue. He was first warned by Peter not to challenge his authority even if he was telling the truth, and he was later warned by a codependent subordinate of Peter that he needed to learn which side his bread was buttered – a thinly veiled threat to do as he was told and not to rock the boat.

Another reason that someone might join a group led by a narcissist is their belief that they might be able to change him. How many women have married, believing that their husband will change when they have the responsibility of looking after children? Some men do change, but they are probably the ones who were not highly narcissistic in the first place. The same applies the other way round, of course: codependent men also marry narcissistic women, believing that they can change them.

Narcissistic leaders of families, work teams, companies or any other grouping continually pressurise their group members to abdicate their individual identity, thought and self-expression in favour of identifying with him (or her), their leader. Codependent wives find themselves unable to make decisions without first consulting their husband. Codependent workers or managers are afraid to take responsibility without first consulting their boss because of fear of how the boss will react if something goes wrong.

Lou Marinoff stated that identification with small groups once favoured human survival and furthered cultural evolution, but paradoxically, such identification has always been a recipe for trouble.[15] This is no doubt true, but not in all cases. There are many small groups such as families, sports teams, work groups and so on that work together happily and continue doing so without ever causing trouble. These groups have leaders, or shared leadership, comprised of normal people who recognise the codependent and narcissistic behaviour of group members and take steps to deal with it. It is the small groups with narcissistic leaders, those who foster 'us' and 'them' relationships with other groups, who cause trouble, or those group members who resent or envy the authority of the 'normal' leader who split the group into factions[16] in order to gain a leadership position of their own.

We already know that the narcissist's success depends on receiving support from a network, typically a group of codependents, possibly combined with narcissists lower down the narcissistic hierarchy. The group then becomes toxic and the troubles begin.

If it's a family, the members are usually led to believe that their family (the 'us') is always right, and that the neighbours (the 'them') are always wrong. The narcissistic leader aggrandises himself and disparages his enemies. If any family member disagrees, he or she is put down in no uncertain terms. Eventually, the 'rogue' family member comes into line and takes on the world view of the narcissist. It is either support the narcissist's view or suffer the consequences.

If it's a work environment, or a sports team, or any other group in which the narcissist is a member, the 'us' and 'them' relationships always come into play; the codependents quickly learn not to threaten the narcissist's ego, any dissidents are brought into line or expelled, and a similar pattern of behaviour to that described in the previous paragraph ensues.

Whilst any of these groups or teams may or may not enjoy success, it is highly unlikely that the membership will feel a sense of real happiness. There will be moments of joy, of humour; there may even be moments of ecstasy, but that true lasting feeling of happiness associated with those who rise from Plato's middle to his top will remain elusive.

If the narcissist is to change, he must first change his view of the world. Instead of viewing himself as being at the centre of the world, he needs to give equal status to important others in his life. This, of course, is difficult, many believe impossible, for a destructive or malignant narcissist. But there are also many families or workgroups that could benefit from a narcissistic member changing the way they view their family members or colleagues, so this is worth striving for.

Take, for example, a father who views his family through the lens of his own mind. Any behaviour that doesn't conform to his beliefs and values, whether right or wrong, he will criticise and correct. If his wife or children object, he will insist that he is right and therefore that they are wrong. In this situation, the father has to rely on the values imbued in him as a child, combined with his own experience of life. He will be challenged by his wife and particularly by his children during their adolescence, but he won't accept their views as he views everything though the subjectivity of his own mind.

An alternative way to view his family is through another, a third party. This means that he accepts that his view of the world is not relevant, and consistently supports the view of the other whom he trusts, in the way that codependents do when viewing the world through the eyes of a narcissist. Historically, this approach has been adopted by many by viewing the world through the discipline imposed by religion – by viewing family behaviour ostensibly through the eyes of God. For example, the Bible and the Koran lay down the values that influence their followers' view of the world, and assistance in any interpretation relating to behaviour can be found by consulting the priest or the imam, or other such religious leader. Unfortunately, the recent decline in religious beliefs, particularly in the western world, has left a vacuum in this area, leaving the narcissist-codependent relationship to flourish, not just through a lack of moral guidance, but also through rampant materialism caused by a media-driven celebrity culture.

The third way for the father to view his family is again through the lens of his own mind, but this time taking a position outside the family and looking in. The family he is looking at includes himself. This way, instead of viewing all interpersonal relationships as how they impact on him, the father, he is able to look at the big picture and view all interpersonal relationships in the family objectively. His values and beliefs are still relevant, but now he is able to see how his behaviour impacts on the other family members, and to recognise that other family members also have values and beliefs that are relevant. His judgements and responses will now be based not on what is best for him, but on what is best for the whole family. By a simple thought modification, the father has now changed the position he views his family from, and he can now appreciate the views of other family members, as well as his own.

There are many families or workgroups that could benefit in this way, from a simple change of perspective. Whilst much of the evidence suggests that the destructive or malignant narcissist will not or cannot change, a majority of narcissistic individuals could benefit from changing the way they view their family members or work colleagues, thus beginning the ascent from Plato's middle to his top. Few people would claim that better interpersonal relations in both the family and the workplace environments will not result in an increase in long-term happiness for all concerned.

11

Nature, Nurture and Boundaries

How Did We Get Here?

'The mind at birth is like a blank slate, waiting to be written on by the world of experience.'[1]

The narcissist exists because of a malfunction of nature and nurture leading to a lack in his knowledge as to where boundaries lie. In Chapter 2 we drew an important distinction between healthy and destructive (or malignant) narcissism.

The healthy narcissist is grounded in a childhood with support for self-esteem and with appropriate limits on behaviour towards others; he has high outward self-confidence in line with reality; he may have a desire for power, wealth and admiration, but it falls within reasonable and acceptable limits; he does not exploit or devalue others, having genuine concern for them and their ideas; and he has values and follows through on plans.

But the unhealthy or malignant narcissist is a completely different person. He is grounded in a traumatic childhood that undercut his true sense of self-esteem and learned that he doesn't need to be considerate of others; he is grandiose and pursues power at all costs, lacking normal inhibitions in its pursuit; in interpersonal relationships his concerns are limited to expressing socially appropriate responses when convenient and with devaluing and exploiting others without remorse; furthermore, he lacks values, consistently failing to follow through on plans, being easily bored and often changing his mind.

Unfortunately, it can be very difficult to differentiate between these two types. The malignant version can be utterly charming, going out of his way to be helpful, always there when needed. In fact, one indication that a malignant narcissist is in the early stages of trapping you into his web of deceit is when he insists on going out of his way to help you. You may well be impressed as he flatters you, making you feel important by appealing to your own narcissistic desires, which we all have, no matter how small they are. This attentive behaviour will go on for as long as it takes to hook you. Thereafter, the degree to which he impacts on your life is dependent upon the extent of his malignancy.

The destructive or malignant narcissist is immoral and unethical. Some of those who have suffered at the hands of a malignant narcissist describe him as evil. Brian Blackwell, for instance, would be described by many in this way.[2] He was diagnosed as having Narcissistic Personality Disorder (NPD)[3] after killing both his parents in 2005, using a claw hammer and a carving knife. He then took his girlfriend on a very expensive holiday to America and Barbados, staying at the best hotels and eating at the best restaurants, paying the bills on his father's credit card.

Blackwell managed to hide the murders for weeks, whilst on holiday and after his return. No one had any idea that his parents' corpses were decomposing in their own home. He continued to deceive, maybe even impress, his girlfriend and her parents, whose home he stayed at on their return from holiday. Kerry Daynes, a consultant forensic psychologist, said, 'The reason why people with NPD are so convincing is that part of them believes it themselves.'[4]

But most of the daily events in our lives that we encounter involving narcissism don't involve horrific crimes, just routine lies, distortion and projection. Should we describe this behaviour as evil? On first thought, most people would probably say no, not evil, it's not as if the narcissist is committing rape – or murder, as in the case of Brian Blackwell.

On the other hand, consider this scenario. Henry, a wealthy father, and his daughter, Charlotte, have a good relationship with each other. Charlotte marries Oliver, a malignant narcissist. After the wedding Oliver has enough money to buy a mid-range car, but wants to buy a luxury car, for which he doesn't have sufficient money, nor can he obtain sufficient credit to make the purchase. So he turns to his father-in-law, Henry, and asks him for a loan. Henry refuses, not wishing his daughter and her new husband to be saddled with debt early in their married life. He points out that a mid-range car without debt is preferable to having a luxury car with debt. The debt needs to be paid back and at the same time it incurs higher costs that are associated with running a more expensive car.

Not surprisingly, Oliver doesn't see it this way. Over time he uses his influence over his wife to distort her perception of her father in order to get back at him, believing that he has suffered a blow to his ego. He undermines her belief in her father's honesty and integrity and drives a wedge between them. This satisfies Oliver's ego, but the loving father-daughter relationship between Henry and Charlotte that existed before is now destroyed.

There has been no crime committed, not in the usual sense of the word. But is Oliver's behaviour evil? Many people would think so. There doesn't even have to be a specific incident such as the refusal of a loan to spark this course of action; it is enough that the narcissist perceives the other person – in this case his father-in-law – to be 'superior' in some way. In this particular example, he is wealthier, and this alone would be sufficient for some narcissists to strike. Brian Blackwell's father was wealthier than him too. His demise was brought about by his refusal to continue financing his narcissistic son's fantasies.

Whilst we differentiated between healthy and malignant narcissism, in reality it is just a question of degree. The malignancy exists even near to the healthy end of the spectrum; it's just that there is only a small dose of it there, and in such a situation it can often be controlled by the victim of the narcissist challenging his behaviour when necessary.

As we discussed in Chapter 8, the behaviour of the narcissist is governed primarily by his unconscious mind. A potential victim can limit the negative impact of the narcissist's malignancy by constantly appealing to his conscious mind to overrule his natural behavioural tendencies. Remember, our unconscious is at the root of all our decisions, not just the big ones, but those innumerable decisions we make on a second-by-second basis. What we think is eventually converted into our actions. So whilst the potential victim can limit the ability of the narcissist to gain control and wreak his evil on her, in practice, she is only delaying such behaviour.

It is likely that the malignant narcissist will never change his behaviour. Many believe that the likelihood of change in his personality disorder ranges from zero to slim. As stated in Chapter 2, Ronningstam and Gunderson noted 'the assiduous and sustained resistance to change common in patients with narcissistic personality disorder'.[5]

The narcissist can't help but respond to prompts that remind him of his underlying feelings of failure and worthlessness. These feelings relate to how he felt during his childhood and the adaptations he had to make to cope with narcissistic parenting figures. According to Dr Alan Rappoport, 'Every narcissistic and co-narcissistic [codependent] person that I have encountered has had narcissistic parents.'[6] The narcissist can't help but respond to trait situational cues, whereby his underlying traits are activated so that the unconscious thoughts that control his behaviour will eventually win through.[7]

It may take days, weeks or months, or it may take many years; the narcissist is quite capable of playing the long game. He remains constant in his behaviour, taking every opportunity to push his distorted world view onto his unsuspecting codependent prey. It is only a matter of time before the victim takes on the distorted world view of her narcissistic oppressor. Then her unconscious, now successfully programmed by the narcissist, stops confronting her oppressor in an assertive way and starts making excuses for his behaviour.

What makes the malignant narcissist particularly evil is that he is parasitic. As he is not able to regulate or soothe himself, he relies on manipulating the external world to provide his sense of self-worth. He is therefore not able to function without hosts, people (codependents) he attaches himself to in order to garner his regular dose of admiration, ego boost, or narcissistic supply.

It has been argued that this is a two-way relationship – the narcissist craves power and offers security and protection in return. But his craving for power means that he has to control his codependent victims, who are in effect imprisoned by him. They will only be released when the narcissist has no further use for them, or when a better opportunity comes his way. This may be never.

The narcissist's craving for power is, on the face of it, aggressive, but in reality, it is defensive. He needs people around him; he is dependent upon them for his survival. He feels threatened by the existence of people outside himself upon whom he depends. His pathological behaviour – treating others as a means to an end, being ruthlessly self-centred, and lacking empathy – are all in fact defences he puts up to avoid being exposed for what he really is – an immoral and unethical being, the result, typically, of constant feelings of self-loathing inculcated into him through narcissistic parenting.

The Calculating Narcissist

Narcissism is a psychological state rooted in extremely low self-esteem.

All narcissists are political beings who have a pathological need to control others. They achieve this by identifying those who can enable them to gain control, be it at a micro level (a small group, his family, a business team, a small company) or at a macro level (a large company or a government). Most of us have personal experience of narcissists taking control at a micro level, and most people with knowledge of history or current affairs are aware of narcissists who have been or who are prominent on the world stage.

Dr Alan Rappoport summarised the behaviour of narcissists, giving the reason why they need to control others, as follows:

Narcissistic people are very fearful of not being well regarded by others, and they therefore attempt to control others' behaviour and viewpoints in order to protect their self-esteem. The underlying dynamic of narcissism is a deep, usually unconscious, sense of oneself as dangerously inadequate and vulnerable to blame and rejection.[8]

Malignant narcissism is a deadly illness, but is different from other deadly illnesses. It's not that the person suffering from it will fall ill and suffer. The narcissist externalises the problem and ensures that others suffer so that he does not. There are many examples of malignant narcissists who have wreaked havoc on their people. Joseph Stalin, Adolf Hitler, Saddam Hussein and Robert Mugabe have already been mentioned as names that immediately spring to mind, but there are many others who have caused and who are continuing to cause endless, unnecessary suffering and destruction. But why do people both at the micro and the macro levels continue to allow their leaders to make them suffer? As Carl Jung said in relation to the Second World War, the German people 'allowed themselves to be driven to the slaughterhouse by their leading psychopaths like hypnotized sheep'.[9]

It is their Machiavellian political cunning and ruthless pursuit of power that enables malignant narcissists to rise to the top in a wide range of environments. And they are able to remain at the top for long periods in many instances, even though a large majority of those under them may be suffering. The narcissist recognises that he only needs to control a relatively small number of key people in order to keep his place at the top.

Take Robert Mugabe, president of Zimbabwe and leader of the Zanu-PF party, for example. After twenty-eight years of his rule the country was on its knees. Despite the best efforts of the opposition party, the Movement for Democratic Change (MDC), and Zimbabwe's neighbours, Mugabe ended up presiding over a country with an inflation rate of 231 million per cent (although quite how that is calculated when there is no food in the shops is anybody's guess), with most of the economically active population (over eighty per cent) being unemployed, and with a huge humanitarian crisis, with five million people in need of food aid, hospitals reporting rising numbers of deaths from malnutrition, a complete breakdown of the country's infrastructure, and a cholera epidemic.

The majority of people wanted him out, but could do nothing about it. Each time crowds protested against the regime, either peacefully or when anger had spilled over onto the streets, they were suppressed. When a crowd of hundreds marched in the capital, Harare, waving placards proclaiming '*Tafa Nenzara*' ('we are dying of hunger'), the police beat back the protesters and arrested them in large numbers.

Mugabe maintained power over the police, army and intelligence services, which became the bedrock of his control. Political commentators estimated that about one per cent of the population continued to live in luxury whilst ninety-nine per cent of the population suffered. The one per cent included Mugabe's inner circle at the Zanu-PF party, and the leaders of the police, the army and the intelligence services. The vast majority of the population endured great hardship but could do nothing in the grip of the narcissistic tyrant. Whilst external political pressure has slightly ameliorated the situation in Zimbabwe, Mugabe still retains power and the country remains in a perilous situation into the second decade of the twenty-first century.

Malignant narcissists in the home and in business adopt the same tactics as Mugabe to control their own small empires, utilising ruthless Machiavellian cunning, an armoury of psychological defences, denial, distortion, splitting and projection. These they apply to their partners, wives or children, or to their colleagues, subordinates or superiors at work, who must take the blame or suffer the consequences. The narcissist can also call upon narcissistic rage, character assassination, abuse and intimidation, not to mention the stealth tactics mentioned in Chapter 2, consisting of name calling, talking down, sexual harassment, disinformation, and using the 'silent treatment'.

But it is splitting which is possibly the most divisive of a narcissist's psychological defences and the one which is most effective in maintaining his control, at the micro level over family or work colleagues, or at the macro level over companies or the government. The narcissist cannot regard people, including groups of people such as political parties, countries, races, and families, as an amalgam of both good and bad elements. To him it is 'all or nothing'. He either idealises his object or devalues it. The object is either all good or all bad.

In the home, for example, this results in a narcissistic father treating his children in different ways. The 'good' child can do no wrong, whereas the 'bad' child is continually punished for behaving badly. In the workplace, subordinates and colleagues are treated in the same way. Political leaders such as Stalin and Hitler took splitting as a means of control to extreme levels. Those considered bad were often executed.

At home, narcissists demand loyalty not to their family, but to themselves. This results in dysfunctional family relationships. At a macro level, where narcissistic leaders of countries demand loyalty, it can result in poor international relations at best, and in the worst cases, war.

'You're either with us or against us' is a phrase usually used to polarise situations and force those being addressed to either become allies or to accept the consequences of being considered an enemy. It is used by narcissists as a defence mechanism to separate a perceived threat into two parts in order to remove its threatening meaning, allowing two separate and contradictory versions of reality to co-exist in their minds. By seeing people or situations in black and white terms, as all bad or all good, the narcissist can avoid the alternative possibilities that may result in a threat to his ego.

For example, the former US president George W. Bush used similar language on more than one occasion during his presidency. He said, 'Either you are with us, or you are with the terrorists' in an address to a joint session of Congress on 20 September 2001. And on 10 January 2002 he said, 'Iran must be a contributor in the war against terror. Our nation and our fight against terror will uphold the doctrine: either you're with us or against us.' An alternative possibility was that Iran and other nations such as France and Russia that didn't follow the line taken by Mr Bush were neither with him nor against him, nor with terrorism. They simply wished to pursue different ways of dealing with terrorism.

These malignant and narcissistic tyrants know what they are doing by employing such tactics, but they just can't stop themselves.

12

The Future

Can We Improve Our Children's Prospects?

'The unexamined life isn't worth living.' [1]

The Good Childhood Inquiry was commissioned by the Children's Society and launched in 2006 as the UK's first independent national inquiry into childhood. The report 'A Good Childhood: Searching for Values in a Competitive Age' was published in 2009 after more than 30,000 people were interviewed in the United Kingdom. It concluded that children today are less happy now than in previous generations, despite society being so much wealthier than ever before.

Children are unhappy through a combination of neglect and parental indulgence. This is as a result of the parents' pursuance of personal success typically through mothers working full time, often solely for materialistic purposes, to 'keep up with the Joneses'. The parents neglect their children because they want the material possessions, the holidays and so on, that their neighbours and colleagues have; or worse still, they want to appear superior to them – for example, to own a better car, to have better holidays – in order to be admired.

The result is that the children are left in front of the television, which acts as a third parent, or in front of the computer, or on games consoles or other gadgets to occupy their time when they are not farmed out to a 'day-orphanage'. This is at the expense of proper social interaction and learning from their parents that they need to grow into rounded adults.

They are then pampered with enormous amounts of material goods and disgusting food by parents who are just assuaging their own guilt. The parents feel guilty because they know that they have neglected their children in pursuit of their own selfish agendas.

The children say that they like 'fast food' – pizza, burgers, ready meals, and the like – and they want to watch television and play on computer games, so the parents claim that they are doing what's right, giving their children what they want, often claiming that they are giving them the things that their own parents couldn't afford to give them. But they are making a fundamental blunder. Children need guidance, input from their parents, who need to show them where the boundaries lie in terms of social interaction, how to react to emotional circumstances, how to deal with failure and difficult situations, how to live morally and ethically. Their error is in mistaking pleasure for happiness.

As the child has been brought up to be materialistic, he needs to have a constant supply of pleasure in order to feel the illusion of happiness, so his demands go on increasing. When the parents should be saying 'no' to the constant demands, their guilt prevents them from doing so, and it is addressed by the parents buying the child even more material possessions and even more junk food, and when he complains that he is still unhappy he is told that he is ungrateful. The parents don't understand why their children are unhappy. They have given them much more than they ever received as children, so surely, they think, they should be both grateful and happy.

The children's desire for more and more material possessions is exacerbated by media pressure (brought about primarily though advertising) and peer pressure; the two feed off each other. The deficiency of proper parenting means that there is no counter to these pressures. The material possessions bring the children transient pleasure, but not happiness. What children really need is the freedom to play and the security of a stable family who interact socially on a daily basis; they need parents who examine their own lives and make decisions based on what is best for the family, not just themselves.

We can see in many adults the consequences of a childhood in which they were set on a path through life involving emotional turmoil and conflict, resulting in feelings of insecurity, inferiority, inadequacy and worthlessness that they believe are their own. In truth, those feelings belonged to their parents, who passed down their repressed problems to them, their children, who in turn had to repress the problems themselves; doing so was the only way they could survive.

When these adults have prejudiced thoughts or make prejudicial and hurtful comments to others, they think that these come from their own conscious thoughts. We have already established in this book that this is not so. They come from their unconscious, which drives their behaviour from thoughts and beliefs implanted in their minds without them even knowing about it. Work by Fionnuala Murphy and others adds to a growing body of research in this area. They looked at how people code moral information and stated:

> Researchers in the area of social cognition have shown that many social psychological phenomena – including attitudes, evaluations and impressions, emotions, and social behaviour – occur automatically and without awareness. The present findings suggest that the same may be true for moral processing.[2]

If we are lucky and have one, or even two, parents who are morally sound, we will have a chance of growing up with a healthy moral and ethical approach to life. If we do not find that in our parents, we only need one person close to us in our childhood, a carer, or a friend or relative, to help point us in the right direction, and give us something to build on, a chance at least.

Later, by examining our own life, we can pick up on those sound inputs we received earlier in our lives and turn them into our beliefs.

We then have the basis for a happy life; by continually examining our lives, we can almost guarantee success as measured on the happiness scale.

We cannot understand why we behave badly by examining our conscious thought if it was corrupted from an early age by our parents, for example, and repressed; it now resides in our unconscious, influencing everything we think and do, but is out of our awareness. However, we *can* examine the symptoms of our behaviour. Our symptoms will tell us what went on in our early life, back even before our earliest memories; when we were about three or four years old in most cases. This was the period in our lives that set us on the path to where we are now, emotionally.

Hannah

'Like a primitive tribal mask, the silent treatment loses all it power to upset you once you refuse to be intimidated.'[3]

Hannah and her husband had been invited by her daughter, Emily, to spend Thanksgiving Day with her and her family. Emily was visiting her husband's family before returning home to meet Hannah and her husband at the agreed time of one o'clock to sit down for Thanksgiving dinner.

Hannah and her husband arrived at their daughter's house on time, but Emily was delayed at her husband's family home. Just as they had been about to leave, in time to return home for one o'clock, other members of her husband's family had arrived. Emily and her family stayed for a while so as not to appear rude, then made their excuses and left as soon as they reasonably could. They arrived home and met Hannah and her husband outside the locked house some twenty minutes late.

Hannah could not disguise her anger. She told her daughter in no uncertain terms that being late was no way to treat her parents. Emily apologised and explained what had happened, but Hannah didn't accept Emily's apology; her simmering rage remained apparent for all to see.

Emily had worked hard to prepare the Thanksgiving dinner for her parents and her family before going out that morning. Later she sat her parents down and served them a wonderful meal. But even at the end of such a magnificently prepared meal, you could cut the atmosphere with a knife.

Hannah gave her daughter the silent treatment. She only spoke when spoken to, and replied typically with one-word answers. This went on for the rest of the afternoon and into the evening. Hannah never lifted a finger to help her daughter all day, and no matter how much Emily tried to please her, waiting on her mother the entire day, it was never enough. Hannah and her husband left during the evening with the atmosphere as cold as it had been since Emily had arrived home twenty minutes late.

Emily visited her mother the following day and apologised profusely for spoiling her day. Hannah eventually accepted Emily's apology. This was clearly not the first time Hannah had controlled her daughter in this way.

Emily accepted the blame for spoiling Thanksgiving Day for her mother. But to any reasonable observer, it should have been Hannah apologising to Emily for spoiling *her* day, as Emily had worked tirelessly to make the day special for her parents, with one minor hiccup that should have been recognised all round as unfortunate. Emily had been groomed by her mother to always take the blame, however, and as a consequence, Hannah used Emily as a dumping ground for her own emotional pain and suffering.

Some time later, Emily was to display the same pattern of behaviour as that of her mother. Emily was a talented clarinet player, and she had a nine-year-old son named Freddie who was already an accomplished saxophonist. One evening when Freddie was playing a piece for his mother at home, she joined in on her clarinet. Freddie was upset as he had wanted to impress his mother, as he had recently perfected his performance of the piece.

Mother and son fell out, but rather than apologise to her son for interrupting his solo piece, or simply explaining that she didn't intend to upset him, she gave him the silent treatment – a form of behaviour clearly learned from her mother. Eventually, Freddie apologised to his mother and begged her forgiveness, as any young child would. It appeared that Freddie was now tainted with the same emotional scars as his mother. The pattern of behaviour has thus been passed down from one generation to the next.

But it is possible to use education, self-examination and the knowledge gained as a consequence to stop dysfunctional patterns of behaviour from being passed down through the generations. Recognition of the problem is the first step towards dealing with it.

The Benefits of Self-examination

'You should examine yourself daily. If you find faults, you should correct them. When you find none, you should try even harder.'[4]

The techniques used to pass down emotional pain and suffering from generation to generation can be identified. Doing so requires a great deal of honesty, and just a small but regular amount of self-examination, as recommended by Socrates. It then becomes possible to apply the knowledge gained to greatly improve our future prospects.

There is little doubt that the examined life makes life more worth living. We can learn from others and from ourselves through the simple steps of observation, thought, study, discussion and reading. Taking these steps will lead us to a better understanding of others, and, perhaps more importantly, it will help us better understand ourselves.

If we can recognise those who are likely to hurt us, such as malignant narcissists, we can avoid them and save ourselves pain and suffering. When we can't avoid them or choose not to, if we can understand how their perverse logic works, how they think, and how they are feeling pain and are suffering, we can take steps to ameliorate both their situation and ours.

When we see others using techniques like denial, projection, character assassination, or the silent treatment, we know that it is they who have a problem, even if we recognise that we also have a problem of our own, but with sufficient knowledge we know that we don't have to take all of the responsibility and pain, as the narcissist intends. And once we feel confident enough to refuse to become attached or be intimidated, we gain the power not to let our emotions cause us mental suffering.

If we can recognise the malignant narcissist who goes out of his way to help us, not for our benefit, but solely for his selfish desire to put himself into a position whereby he has control over us, we can avoid being snared by his cunning behaviour. Through self-examination we can recognise the part we play in the deception, and then we can take action to avoid future emotional pain and suffering.

Understanding what the great thinkers throughout history have taught us can contribute to our knowledge of human behaviour. The theory and practice relating to Stoicism, for instance, gives us a means to gain power over ourselves. The central concepts of Stoicism are being able to grit your teeth, so to speak, in distressing situations and, more importantly, to value only that which no one can take from you. If we place value on things like virtue, instead of material possessions, for instance, we put ourselves in a position where no one has power over us.

As we live in a society that seems to be becoming more and more materialistic, it is even more important to understand these concepts in order to give us the tools we need to steer clear of the emotional pain and suffering caused by narcissists and codependents.

Notes and References

Chapter 1: What's the Problem?

1. From Shakespeare's *As You Like It*.
2. For details on Zimbardo's Stanford University 1971 prison study, see C. Haney, W .C. Banks and P. G. Zimbardo (1973), 'A Study of Prisoners and Guards in a Simulated Prison', *Naval Research Review*, 30, pp. 4-17.
3. The historian and moralist John Emerich Edward Dalberg Acton, first Baron Acton (1834–1902), who was otherwise known simply as Lord Acton, expressed this opinion in a letter to Bishop Mandell Creighton in 1887: 'Power tends to corrupt, and absolute power corrupts absolutely. Great men are almost always bad men.'
4. See Chapter 2, under 'Can You Recognise a Narcissist?' for a definition of 'projection'.

Chapter 2: Narcissism

1. Self-esteem is the degree to which one values oneself, and also encompasses faith in oneself, pride, self-assurance, self-regard, self-respect and vanity.
2. Neurosis is characterised by anxiousness, worrying, moodiness and frequent depression, and is linked to obsessive behaviour. The psychologist Carl Rogers described neurosis as the gap between the real self and the ideal self, or between the 'I am' and the 'I should'. The greater the gap, the more suffering for the neurotic.
3. Paranoia is a functional disorder characterised by delusions of either

grandeur and/or persecution, which can't be explained by other psychological disorders. Intellectual functioning is not impaired. The paranoid is quite capable of coherent behaviour within his or her delusional state. Narcissists always suffer from paranoia.

4. Narcissists suffer from narcissism. It relates to an exceptional interest in or admiration of oneself, especially concerning one's physical appearance or mental endowments.

5. Manfred Kets de Vries (2003), 'The Dark Side of Leadership', *Business Strategy Review*, 14(3), Autumn, p. 26.

6. See Barbera Engler (2003), *Personality Theories: An Introduction*, 6th ed. (New York: Houghton Mifflin), pp. 99–107.

7. Envy is a feeling or an emotional state of grudging or admiring discontent aroused by the possessions, achievements, or qualities of another, involving the desire to have for oneself something possessed by another; it is covetousness. Envy is usually linked to narcissism, paranoia and projection (or projective identification), and tends to be evident in varying degrees in all narcissists. It always involves making a comparison – we envy what we don't have. A common method used by narcissists to get rid of the painful emotion of envy is to use projection, or projective identification. The narcissist projects the feelings that he does not want to have onto the person he envies – that is, onto the object of his envy. For example, a narcissist who is envious of a better-qualified colleague at work may greatly exaggerate and publicise minor failures by his colleague, and at the same time ignore or greatly understate his successes.

8. S. Vaknin (1999), *Malignant Self Love: Narcissism Revisited* (Skopje: Narcissus Publications).

9. The terms 'codependent' (e.g. A. Wilson-Schaef [1987], *When Society Becomes an Addict* [San Francisco: Harper & Row]), 'enabler' (A. Downs [1997], *Beyond the Looking Glass: Overcoming the Seductive Culture of Corporate Narcissism* [New York: AMACOM]), 'follower' (D. Sandowski [1995], 'The Charismatic Leader as Narcissist: Understanding the Abuse of Power', *Organizational Dynamics*, 23(4), pp. 57–71), 'covert narcissist' (e.g. A. Lowen [1997], *Narcissism: Denial of the True Self* [New York: Touchstone Books]), 'inverted narcissist' (S. Vaknin [1997–2005]), *Malignant Self Love: Narcissism Revisited* [Skopje and Prague: Narcissus Publications]), and 'co-narcissist' (Alan Pappoport [2005, in press], 'Co-narcissism: How We Accommodate to Narcissistic

Parents', *The Therapist*) are used interchangeably in respect of people who are emotionally dependent on narcissists. Narcissists surround themselves with codependents as the latter tend to work beyond healthy (and sometimes ethical) limits to do whatever the narcissist needs them to do. Narcissists crave power and codependents crave security, so they are drawn to one another. Codependency was initially referenced in the literature in relation to the codependents of alcoholics, but it has more recently been used in a wider context, including for the codependents of narcissists. It is a condition that affects a large percentage of the adult population. Codependent patterns of behaviour vary in degree from individual to individual, but include, among other characteristics:

- Avoiding decision making and confrontation
- External referencing (always checking outside oneself before making choices)
- Subordinating one's needs to those of the person with whom one is involved (i.e. the narcissist)
- Perfectionism
- Over-control
- Manipulation
- Lack of trust
- Lying

10. See S. B. Robbins and P. Dupont (1992), 'Narcissistic Needs of the Self and Perceptions of Interpersonal Behaviour', *Journal of Counselling Psychology*, 39(2), pp. 462–67.

11. See M. Maccoby (2000), 'Narcissistic Leaders: The Incredible Pros, the Inevitable Cons', *Harvard Business Review*, January-February, p. 75.

12. See A. Downs (1997), *Beyond the Looking Glass: Overcoming the Seductive Culture of Corporate Narcissism* (New York: AMACOM).

13. Narcissistic rage, as the name suggests, occurs when a narcissist goes into a rage. This happens when the narcissist suffers a psychological wounding of his essential self. Such a blow to his core identity will typically lower his self-esteem and produce feelings of humiliation, shame and rage.

14. See O. Kernberg (1992), *Borderline Conditions and Pathological Narcissism* (New York: Jason Aronson).

15. Quotation from L. M. Bogart, E. G. Benotsh and J. D. Pavlovic (2004), 'Feeling Superior but Threatened: The Relation of Narcissism

to Social Comparison', *Basic and Applied Social Psychology*, 26(1), pp. 35–44.

16. See, for example, W. K. Campbell, A. S. Goodie and J. D. Foster (2004), 'Narcissism, Confidence, and Risk Attitude', *Journal of Behavioural Decision Making*, 17, pp. 297–311.

17. W. K. Campbell, J. D. Foster and A. B. Brunell (2004), 'Running from Shame or Revelling in Pride? Narcissism and Regulation of Self-Conscious Emotions', *Psychological Inquiry*, 15(2), pp. 150–53.

18. A. Reich (1933), *Character-Analysis* (New York: Noonday Press).

19. Character assassination is an intentional attempt, usually by a narcissist and/or codependent, to influence the portrayal or reputation of someone in such a way as to cause others to develop an extremely negative or unappealing perception of him or her. It typically involves deliberate exaggeration or manipulation of facts, the spreading of rumours and deliberate misinformation to present an untrue picture of the targeted person, and unwarranted and excessive criticism.

20. Projection, also called projective identification, involves the tendency to see your own unacceptable desires in other people. In other words, the desires are still there, but they're not your desires any more. The objective is to make you feel superior. An important motive for projection lies in the desire of the 'projector' to control the person who is reminding them of their low self-esteem, or feelings of inferiority, inadequacy and worthlessness, to prevent him or her from making the 'projector' feel bad (M. Klein [1975], *Envy and Gratitude and Other Works 1946–1963* [London: Hogarth Press and the Institute of Psycho-Analysis]). Projective identification may be differentiated from projection when the individual does not completely disavow what is projected. Instead, the person remains aware of his or her own feelings or emotions, but misattributes them and regards them as being justifiable reactions to the behaviour of the other person (A. S. Reber [1995], *Dictionary of Psychology*, 2nd ed. [Harmondsworth: Penguin]).

21. N. McWilliams and S. Lependorf (1990), 'Narcissistic Pathology of Everyday Life: The Denial of Remorse and Gratitude', *Contemporary Psychoanalysis*, 26(3), pp. 430–51.

22. A. D. Brown (1997), 'Narcissism, Identity, and Legitimacy', *Academy of Management Review*, 22(3), pp. 643–86.

23. Ego psychology relates to ego processes such as memory, language, judgement, decision-making and other reality-oriented functions.

24. Object relations are the emotional bonds between oneself and another, typically expressed in the sense of one's capacity to love and care for another as balanced against interest in and love for the self.

25. O. Kernberg (1992), *Borderline Conditions and Pathological Narcissism* (New York: Jason Aronson).

26. R. Lubit (2002), 'The Long-term Organisational Impact of Destructively Narcissistic Managers', *Academy of Management Executive*, 16(1), pp. 127–38.

27. Mirroring is a theory developed by Heinz Kohut whereby children have their talk and accomplishments acknowledged, accepted and praised by others – for example, by parents. It is important for a child's legitimate feelings of grandiosity to be mirrored by his or her parents. Children who do not get enough mirroring (admiration, attention, etc.) are considered by many psychologists to be at risk of developing a narcissistic personality later in life. The parents' mirroring gets internalised in time, so as the child gets older he (or she) can provide his own mirroring, his own sense of self-appreciation. The basis of healthy self-esteem is that one's natural self, with all its emotions, with its successes and failures, is acceptable and loveable. If the child does not feel that his parents love him for himself, apart from his accomplishments, he will develop what object relations theorists call the 'false self', the self that is fabricated in order to get the approval of his parents, based on the ability to achieve good grades, a good job, a good mate, etc. Pathological narcissism is a result of faulty self-development and results in the narcissist presenting a false self, constantly 'mirroring' himself (or herself) against others.

28. Vaknin (1997–2005).

29. A. Downs (1997), *Beyond the Looking Glass: Overcoming the Seductive Culture of Corporate Narcissism*, AMACOM, New York.

30. For example, Campbell, Goodie and Foster (2004).

31. S. Vazire and D. C. Funder (2006), 'Impulsivity and the Self-Defeating Behavior of Narcissists', *Personality and Social Psychology Review*, 10(2), pp. 154–65.

32. See Downs (1997).

33. For example, R. P. Tett and H. A. Guterman (2000), 'Situation Trait Relevance, Trait Expression, and Cross-situational Consistency: Testing a Principle of Trait Activation', *Journal of Research in Personality*, 34, pp. 397–423.

34. See Downs (1997).
35. P. J. Watson, S. E. Hickman, R. J. Morris, J. T. Milliron and L. Whiting (1995), 'Narcissism, Self-Esteem, and Parental Nurturance', *Journal of Psychology*, 129(1), pp. 69–73.
36. R. D. Chessick (1985), *Psychology of the Self and the Treatment of Narcissism* (Northvale, NJ: Jason Aronson).
37. See Watson et al. (1995).
38. J. R. Buri, P. Murphy, L. M. Richtsmeier and K. K. Komar (1992), 'Stability of Parental Nurturance as a Salient Predictor of Self-esteem', *Psychological Reports*, 71, pp. 535–43.
39. M. Maccoby (2000), 'Narcissistic Leaders: The Incredible Pros, the Inevitable Cons', *Harvard Business Review*, January-February, p. 75.
40. See http://ceres.ca.gov/tcsf/pathways/chapter12.html.
41. See http://ceres.ca.gov/tcsf/pathways/chapter12.html.
42. D. Sankowsky (1995), 'The Charismatic Leader as Narcissist: Understanding the Abuse of Power', *Organisational Dynamics*, 23(4), pp. 57–71 (p. 63).
43. Splitting is a Freudian defence mechanism in which an object or idea (or, alternatively, the ego) is separated into two or more parts in order to remove its threatening meaning. Freud referred to splitting as a mental process by which two separate and contradictory versions of reality could co-exist. This conceptualisation of splitting defines an ego that allows reality to be both acknowledged and denied. Splitting is a defence mechanism present in all narcissists. They see people and situations in black-and-white terms, all bad or all good, with no shades of grey.
44. See http://ceres.ca.gov/tcsf/pathways/chapter12.html.
45. Quotation from J. Holmes (2001), *Ideas in Psychoanalysis: Narcissism* (Cambridge: Icon Books), p. 57.
46. M. Golomb, M. Fava, M. Abraham and J. F. Rosenbaum (1995), 'Gender Differences in Personality Disorders', *American Journal of Psychiatry*, 152(4), pp. 579–582.
47. A. Ramsey, P. J. Watson, M. D. Biderman and A. L. Reeves (1996), 'Self-reported Narcissism and Perceived Parental Permissiveness and Authoritarianism', *Journal of Genetic Psychology*, 157(2), pp. 227–238.
48. See Ramsey et al. (1996).
49. See Ramsey et al. (1996).

50. L. Imbesi (1999), 'The Making of a Narcissist', *Clinical Social Work Journal*, 27, pp. 41–54.
51. C. Glickauf-Haughes (1997), 'Etiology of the Masochistic and Narcissistic Personality', *American Journal of Psychoanalysis*, 57, pp. 141–48.
52. See Imbesi (1999).
53. A. Lowen, MD (1983), *Narcissism: Denial of the True Self* (New York: MacMillan).
54. H. Kohut (1971), *The Analysis of the Self* (New York: International Universities Press).
55. E. Bleiber (1994), 'Normal and Pathological Narcissism in Adolescence', *American Journal of Psychotherapy*, 48, pp. 30–45.
56. See Ramsey et al. (1996).
57. G. C. Davison and J. M. Neale (2001), *Abnormal Psychology*, 8th ed. (New York: Wiley).
58. Quotation from D. Bell (2002), *Ideas in Psychoanalysis: Paranoia* (Cambridge: Icon Books), p. 57.
59. Narcissistic Personality Disorder (NPD) is a mental disorder. The *Diagnostic and Statistical Manual of Mental Disorders* (DSM), published by the American Psychiatric Association, is the handbook used most often in diagnosing mental disorders in the United States and internationally. The *International Statistical Classification of Diseases and Related Health Problems* (ICD) is a commonly used alternative. Narcissistic Personality Disorder as defined by the DSM (Diagnostic Criteria DSM-IV-TR) is characterised by a pervasive pattern of grandiosity (in fantasy or behaviour), a need for admiration, and a lack of empathy, beginning by early adulthood and present in a variety of contexts, as indicated by five (or more) of the following:

I. has a grandiose sense of self-importance (e.g. exaggerates achievements and talents, expects to be recognised as superior without commensurate achievements);
II. is preoccupied with fantasies of unlimited success, power, brilliance, beauty, or ideal love;
III. believes that he or she is 'special' and 'unique' and can only be understood by, or should associate with, other special or high-status people (or institutions);
IV. requires excessive admiration;
V. has a sense of entitlement (i.e. unreasonable expectations of

especially favourable treatment or automatic compliance with his or her expectations);

VI. is interpersonally exploitative (i.e. takes advantage of others to achieve his or her own ends);

VII. lacks empathy: is unwilling to recognise or identify with the feelings and needs of others;

VIII. is often envious of others or believes that others are envious of him or her;

IX. shows arrogant, haughty behaviours or attitudes.

60. For example, A. Travers (1989), 'Shelf-Life Zero: A Classic Postmodernist Paper', *Philosophy of the Social Sciences*, 19(3), pp. 291–320.

61. Campbell, Goodie and Foster (2004).

62. Belbin's leadership team roles, strengths and styles are described as follows (see R. M. Belbin [1981], *Management Teams: Why They Succeed or Fail* [London: Heinemann]):

Coordinator (CO): Able to get others working to a shared aim; confident, mature (originally called 'Chairman' by Belbin).

Shaper (SH): Motivated, energetic, achievement-driven, assertive, competitive.

63. R. Lubit (2002), 'The Long-term Organisational Impact of Destructively Narcissistic Managers', *Academy of Management Executive*, 16(1), pp. 127–38.

64. Belbin (1981).

65. Kets de Vries (2003), p. 26.

66. E. Ronningstam and J. Gunderson (1996), 'Narcissistic Personality: A Stable Disorder or a State of Mind?' *Psychiatric Times*, 12(2), pp. 35–36.

67. T. Millon. (1998), 'DSM Narcissistic Personality Disorder', in *Disorders of Narcissism: Diagnostic, Clinical, and Empirical Implications*, ed. Elsa F. Ronningstam, p. 75 (Washington, DC: American Psychiatric Press).

68. T. Millon and R. Davis (2000), *Personality Disorders in Modern Life* (New York: Wiley), p. 294.

69. O. Kernberg (1985), *Internal World and External Reality* (New York: Jason Aronson); O. Kernberg (1992), *Borderline Conditions and Pathological Narcissism* (New York: Jason Aronson).

70. J. J. McDonald (2005), 'The Narcissistic Plaintiff', *Employee Relations Law Journal*, 30(4), p. 97.

71. G. C. Davison and J. M. Neale (2001), *Abnormal Psychology*, 8th ed. (New York: Wiley).

72. Aristotle, *The Art of Rhetoric*, (Translated by Hugh Lawson-Tancred, Reissue edition 27 Jan 2005) (London: Penguin Classics), p. 170.
73. K. Barrows (2002), *Ideas in Psychoanalysis: Envy* (Cambridge: Icon Books), p. 11.
74. Robert Frank (2007), *Falling Behind: How Rising Inequality Harms the Middle Class* (Berkeley: University of California Press).

Chapter 3: Codependency

1. J. A. Hogg and L. Frank (1992), 'Towards an Interpersonal Model of Codependence and Contradependence', *Journal of Counseling & Development*, 70, pp. 371–75.
2. J. Friel and L. Freil (1988), *Adult Children: The Secrets of Dysfunctional Families* (Deerfield Beach, FL: Health Communications).
3. J. Laign (1989), 'A Consensus on Codependency', *Contact*, 2(2), p. 2.
4. D. Lyon and J. Greenberg (1991), 'Evidence of Codependency in Women with an Alcoholic Parent: Helping Out Mr Wong', *Journal of Personality and Social Psychology*, 3, pp. 435–39.
5. See Chapter 2, n.9 for a definition of all of these terms.
6. Melody Beattie (1992), *Codependent No More: How to Stop Controlling Others and Start Caring for Yourself* (Center City, MN: Hazelden), pp. 37–8.
7. J. A. Hogg and L. Frank (1992), 'Towards an Interpersonal Model of Codependence and Contradependence', *Journal of Counseling & Development*, 70, pp. 371–75.
8. See Hogg and Frank (1992).
9. R. Baker and S. Newport (2003), 'Dysfunctional Managerial Behaviour in the Workplace: Implications for Employees, Supervisors, and Organisations', *Problems and Perspectives of Management*, 1, pp. 108–13.
10. F. S. Hall (1991), 'Dysfunctional Managers: The Next Human Resource Challenge', *Organisational Dynamics*, 20, pp. 48–57.
11. Quotation from R. A. Cook and J. L. Goff (2002), 'Coming of Age with Self-managed Teams: Dealing with a Problem Employee', *Journal of Business and Psychology*, 16(3), pp. 485–96.
12. Baker and Newport (2003).
13. See Cook and Goff (2002).
14. See Cook and Goff (2002).

15. See Cook and Goff (2002).
16. C. A. Whitfield (1992), *Co-dependence, Addictions, and Related Disorders: A Comprehensive Textbook*, 2nd ed., ed. J. H. Lowinson, P. Ruiz, R. B. Millman, and J. G. Langrod, pp. 816–31 (Baltimore, MD: Williams & Wilkins).
17. T. L. Cermak (1986), *Diagnosing and Treating Co-dependence* (Minneapolis: Johnson Institute).
18. See Cook and Goff (2002).
19. Dr. Stan J. Katz and Aimee E. Liu (1991), *The Codependency Conspiracy* (New York: Warner Books).

Chapter 4: Leadership

1. Authoritarian (or autocratic) leadership is characterised by intolerance of difference and challenge. It requires, above all, obedience and conformity.
2. M. Van Vugt, S. Jepson, C. Hart and D. De Cremer (2004), 'Autocratic Leadership in Social Dilemmas: A Threat to Group Stability', *Journal of Experimental Social Psychology*, 40(1), pp. 1–13.
3. D. J. Storey (1994), *Understanding the Small Business Sector* (London: International Thompson Business Press); B. J. Orser, S. Hogarth-Scott and A. L. Riding (2000), 'Performance, Firm Size, and Management Problem Solving', *Journal of Small Business Management*, 38(4), pp. 42–59.
4. S. Cromie and I. Callaghan (1997) 'Assessing Enterprise Attributes: The Usefulness of Caird's General Enterprising Tendency (GET) Test', *Small Business and Enterprise Development*, 4, pp. 65–71; R. Lessem and Y. Baruch (2000), 'Testing the SMT and Belbin Inventories in Top Management Teams', *Leadership & Organisation Development Journal*, 21(2), pp. 75–84.
5. M. Maccoby (2000), 'Narcissistic Leaders: The Incredible Pros, the Inevitable Cons, *Harvard Business Review*, January-February, p. 75.
6. Kets de Vries (2003), p. 26.
7. Belbin (1981).
8. See, for example, S. Vyakarnam, R. C. Jacobs and J. Handelberg (1999), 'Exploring the Formation of Entrepreneurial Teams: The Key to Rapid Growth Business?' *Journal of Small Business and Enterprise Development*, 6(2), pp. 153–65.

9. M. F. R. Kets de Vries (1985), 'Narcissism and Leadership: An Object Relations Perspective', *Human Relations*, 38, pp. 583–601.
10. Obsessive behaviour is linked to neurosis and is characterised by anxiousness, worrying, moodiness, and frequent depression. Neurosis is the gap between the real self and the ideal self, or the 'I am' and the 'I should'. The greater the gap, the more suffering is involved for the neurotic.
11. A. A. Cannella and M. J. Monroe (1997), 'Contrasting Perspectives on Strategic Leaders: Toward a More Realistic View of Top Managers', *Journal of Management*, 23(3), pp. 213–37.
12. See Chapter 2, n.59, for diagnostic criteria for Narcissistic Personality Disorder (DSM-IV-TR).
13. D. K. Thomas, W. D. Murphy and G. Fearn (2001), 'Analysis of Senior Management Teams in Growth and Lifestyle SMEs', 24th ISBA National Small Firms Policy and Research Conference, Leicester, *Conference Proceedings*, 1, pp. 433–52.
14. See Thomas, Murphy and Fearn (2001)
15. The 'Job Choice Decision-Making Exercise' (JCE) by Michael J. Stahl and Anil Gulati measures need for achievement, power, and affiliation. It is based primarily on the work by D. C. McClelland. The 'Entrepreneurial Style and Success Indicator' (ESSI) by Howard L. Shenson, Terry D. Anderson, Jonathan Clark and Susan Clark claims to assess variables thought to be related to entrepreneurial success and to increase understanding of entrepreneurial style. It measures behavioural action, cognitive analysis, interpersonal harmony and affective expression, along with twenty-eight 'success factors'. The 'EQ Questionnaire' by Edward J. Fasiska is designed to measure entrepreneurial and executive effectiveness, and to be used as a personal and organisational development tool. It measures adaptability, managerial traits (risk tolerance, time management, creativity, strategic thinking, planning, goal orientation), personality traits (extroversion, intuition, thinking, perceiving), and the EQ (Entrepreneurial Quotient) index.
16. A. S. King (1985), 'Self-analysis and Assessment of Entrepreneurial Potential', *Simulations and Games*, 16(4), pp. 397–416.
17. J. Freeley (1986), *Entrepreneurial Style Profile* (New York: Long Island University). Comparison of the King and Freeley instruments against the main characteristics associated with enterprise tendency reveals

167

that neither instrument meets the specified criteria for accurate measurement. King's 'Behavioural Checklist' addresses locus of control and risk taking, and need for achievement is addressed by achievement and motivation measures. It could also be argued that creativity is addressed by the instruments measuring problem-solving ability and manipulative skills. However, it does not address need for autonomy. Freeley's 'Entrepreneurial Style' instrument measures risk taking, and it could also be argued that it addresses need for achievement with the motivation instrument, need for autonomy with the independence instrument, and creativity with the problem-solving and variety instruments, but it does not address locus of control.

18. See, for example, S. Cromie and I. Callaghan (1997), 'Assessing Enterprise Attributes: The Usefulness of Caird's General Enterprising Tendency (GET) Test', *Small Business and Enterprise Development*, 4, pp. 65–71.

Chapter 5: Teamwork

1. John Donne was an English clergyman and poet (1572–1631). The quotation in full is: 'No man is an Island, entire of itself; every man is a piece of the Continent, a part of the main; if a clod be washed away by the sea, Europe is the less, as well as if a promontory were, as well as if a manor of thy friends or of thine own were; any man's death diminishes me, because I am involved in Mankind; And therefore never send to know for whom the bell tolls; It tolls for thee' (Meditation XVII).
2. Belbin (1981).
3. See Belbin (1981).
4. M. E. Mangelsdorf (1992), 'The Inc. 500: America's Fastest Growing Private Companies', *Inc.*, 14(10), pp. 71–80; L. Brockaw (1993), 'The Truth about Start-Ups', *Inc.*, 15(3), pp. 56–64.
5. S. Vyakarnam, R. C. Jacobs and J. Handelberg (1999), 'Exploring the Formation of Entrepreneurial Teams: The Key to Rapid Growth Business?' *Journal of Small Business and Enterprise Development*, 6(2), pp. 153–65.
6. See D. K. Thomas, W. D. Murphy and G. Fearn (2001).
7. S. Freud (1940), *Splitting of the Ego in the Process of Defence*, standard ed., vol. 23, pp. 271–78 (London: Hogarth Press).

8. R. Lubit (2002), 'The Long-term Organisational Impact of Destructively Narcissistic Managers', *Academy of Management Executive*, 16(1), p. 132.
9. D. Gilbert (2006), *Stumbling on Happiness* (London: HarperCollins).
10. Gilbert (2006).
11. J. Holmes (2001), *Ideas in Psychoanalysis: Narcissism* (Cambridge: Icon Books), p. 57.
12. G. R. Loftus and E. F. Loftus (1975), *Human Memory: The Processing of Information* (New York: Halsted Press), cited in *Foundations of Psychology, An Introductory Text*, ed. N. Hayes, 2nd ed. (London: Thomas Nelson).
13. T. Millon and R. Davis (2000), *Personality Disorders in Modern Life* (New York: Wiley), p. 294.
14. Gilbert (2006), p.206.

Chapter 6: A Narcissistic Team Member

1. Not the real name of the consultancy organisation.
2. Belbin (1981). The following describe some of Belbin's team roles, in terms of strengths and styles: Team Worker (TW) – team role is one who is supportive, sociable, flexible, adaptable, perceptive, a listener, with a calming influence, a mediator. Implementer (IMP) – team role is one who is systematic, has common sense, is loyal, structured, reliable, dependable, practicable, efficient (originally called 'Company Worker'). Shaper (SH) – team role is one who is motivated, energetic, achievement-driven, assertive, competitive. Coordinator (CO) – team role is one who is able to get others working to a shared aim; confident, mature.
3. See n.2.

Chapter 7: The Narcissist at Work

1. Susie Orbach, psychoanalyst and writer, quoted in the *Guardian* and *Observer* newspapers guide booklet, 'How to Understand People', part 1, March 2009, p. 5.
2. See John Gottman, Robert Levenson and Erica Woodin (2001), 'Facial Expressions During Marital Conflict', *Journal of Family Communication*, 1(1), pp. 37–57.

3. A. D. Brown (1997), 'Narcissism, Identity, and Legitimacy', *Academy of Management Review*, 22(3), p. 661.
4. For a definition of 'character assassination', see Chapter 2, n.19.
5. Howard S. Schwartz (1987), 'On the Psychodynamics of Organizational Totalitarianism', *Journal of Management*, 13(1), p. 51.
6. Alice Miller (2008; originally published in 1979), *The Drama of the Gifted Child* (New York: Basic Books). The word 'gifted' in the title simply means those who have survived an abusive childhood thanks to an ability to adapt even to unspeakable cruelty.
7. From blog by 'George U.X.' at http://libspirit.blogspot.com.
8. From poem by Philip Larkin, an English poet, novelist and jazz critic commonly regarded as one of the greatest English poets of the latter half of the twentieth century. The full poem is:

They f*** you up, your mum and dad
They may not mean to, but they do.
They fill you with the faults they had
And add some extra, just for you.

But they were f***ed up in their turn
By fools in old-style hats and coats,
Who half the time were soppy-stern
And half at one another's throats.

Man hands on misery to man
It deepens like a coastal shelf.
Get out as early as you can
And don't have any kids yourself.

9. See Miller (2008 [1979]).
10. Lou Marinoff (2003), *The Big Questions: How Philosophy Can Change Your Life* (New York: Bloomsbury), p. 52. Marinoff is a professor of philosophy at the City College of New York and a philosophical counsellor (p. 52).
11. From Marinoff (2003), p. 41.

NOTES AND REFERENCES

Chapter 8: Trust and Loyalty

1. Stoicism is an ancient Greek philosophy that teaches the development of self-control and fortitude as a means of overcoming destructive emotions. It is thought to improve the individual's ethical and moral well-being.
2. Manson, Jennifer (2008), 'Survival of the nastiest', *New Scientist*, 199, pp. 20–21.
3. Transference is the redirection of attitudes and emotions towards a substitute. For example, an employee may see his manager as a father figure (paternal transference), especially if the employee had a difficult relationship with his father during childhood. Typically, the pattern projected onto the other person comes from a childhood relationship. This may be from an actual person, such a parent, or from an idealised figure. It involves the transfer of power and also expectation: 'If you treat me as a parent, I can tell you what to do, but you will also expect me to care for you.' This can have both positive and negative outcomes. Narcissistic managers actively seek subordinates who treat them as a parent figure through transference. They then assume wisdom, and speak with authority. They reassure their subordinates that all will be well if they do as they are told. This makes the narcissistic manager feel good (childlike respect and admiration gives them a boost to their fluctuating self-esteem), and gives them power. For male narcissistic managers, this is known as paternal transference, and for female narcissistic managers, it is known as maternal transference. The narcissistic manager uses the power of his or her position of authority to provide protection and control in return for loyalty and obedience. Note, however, that transference and projection are different. Transference is activated in the person, probably through unmet emotional needs as a child, and projection is caused by the transference; it involves the release of that transference out of the person.
4. Josiah Royce (1855–1916), an American philosopher.
5. Christopher Lasch (1979), *The Culture of Narcissism: American Life in an Age of Diminishing Expectations* (New York: Norton), p. 23.

171

Chapter 9: Morals and Ethics

1. See Marinoff (2003).
2. Alain de Botton (2000), *The Consolations of Philosophy* (London: Penguin Books), p. 55.
3. De Botton (2000), p. 55.
4. Anthony O'Hear (2006), *Plato's Children: The State We Are In* (London: Gibson Square), p. 225.
5. See Marinoff (2003).
6. Soren Kierkegaard (1992), *Either/or: A Fragment of Life*, Translated by Alastair Hannay, (London: Penguin Books). *Either/Or* is recognised by many as Kierkegaard's greatest work. It sets out a view of two modes of life, the 'aesthetic' and the 'ethical'.
7. Quotation is from an unknown source. It is commonly attributed to 'Frank Outlaw' on various websites, but there is no evidence to confirm that this is the correct source.
8. Dr Benjamin Libet has written the following works: 'Neuronal vs. Subjective Timing, for a Conscious Sensory Experience', in *Cerebral Correlates of Conscious Experience*, ed. P. A. Buser and A Rogeul-Buser (Amsterdam/New York: North Holland, 1978), pp. 69–82; 'Unconscious Cerebral Initiative and the Role of Conscious Will in Voluntary Action', *Behavioural and Brain Sciences*, 8 (1985), pp 529–66; 'Do We have Free Will?' *Journal of Consciousness Studies*, 6 (1999), pp. 47–58.
9. Susan Pockett (2002), 'On Subjective Back-referral and How Long it Takes to become Conscious of a Stimulus: A Reinterpretation of Libet's Data', *Consciousness and Cognition*, 11, p. 144.

Chapter 10: Happiness

1. Marcus Aurelius, (AD 121–180) *Meditations* (or *Writings to Himself*). The quotation in full is: 'The happiness of your life depends on the quality of your thoughts; therefore, guard accordingly, and take care that you entertain no notions unsuitable to virtue and reasonable nature.'
2. André Comte-Sponville (2005), *The Little Book of Philosophy* (London: Vintage Books), p. 27.
3. Comte-Sponville (2005), p. xvii.
4. O'Hear (2006).

5. Alan Rappoport (2005), 'Co-narcissism: How We Accommodate to Narcissistic Parents', *The Therapist*, in press (see www.alanrappoport. com).
6. Desmond Lee, trans. (2003), *Plato: The Republic*, 2nd ed. (London: Penguin Books), p. 325.
7. Lee (2003), p. 300.
8. Margie E. Lachman, Christina Röcke, Christopher Rosnick and Carol D. Ryff (2008), 'Realism and Illusion in Americans' Temporal Views of their Life Satisfaction: Age Differences in Reconstructing the Past and Anticipating the Future', *Psychological Science*, 19(9), pp. 889–97.
9. See n.6, pp. 325–26.
10. Marinoff (2003), p. 196.
11. From Plato's *Republic* (see above, Chapter 10, n.6, p. 52).
12. Kets de Vries (2003), p. 26.
13. Miller (2008 [1979]), p. 42.
14. Amanda C. Brandone and Henry M. Wellman (2009), 'You Can't Always Get What You Want: Infants Understand Failed Goal-directed Actions', *Psychological Science*, 20(1), pp. 85–91.
15. Marinoff (2003), p. 196.
16. See Chapter 2, n.43 for definition of 'splitting'.

Chapter 11: Nature, Nurture and Boundaries

1. John Locke (1632–1704), from his *Second Treatise on Civil Government*. He describes the mind at birth as a blank slate (tabula rasa) that is filled later through experience.
2. The court case relating to Brian Blackwell was reported in the *Sunday Times* magazine on 9 October 2005, pp. 22–28.
3. See Chapter 2, n.59.
4. From the *Sunday Times* magazine – see n.2 above.
5. Ronningstam and Gunderson (1996).
6. See Rappoport (2005).
7. The principle of trait activation goes back to 1938 when Henry Murray suggested that situations exert 'press' on individuals to behave in trait-related ways. The concept of 'situational trait relevance' is based on this idea. Thus, if one wishes to assess nurturance, for example, one must observe people in situations where nurturance is a viable

response. A situation is relevant to a trait if it is thematically connected by the provision of cues, responses (or lack of responses) to which indicate a person's standing on the trait (Robert P. Tett and Dawn D. Burnett [2003], 'A Personality Trait-based Interactionist Model of Job Performance', *Journal of Applied Psychology*, 88[3], pp. 500–17).

8. Rappoport (2005).
9. Carl Jung (1970), *Civilization in Transition*, in *The Collected Works of C. G. Jung*, vol. 10, 2nd ed. (Princeton, NJ: Princeton University Press).

Chapter 12: The Future

1. Quoted by Socrates, written by Plato. See Harold North Fowler, trans. (1966), *Plato in Twelve Volumes*, vol. 1 (London: Heinemann).
2. Fionnuala Murphy, Gemma Wilde, Neil Ogden, Philip Barnard and Andrew Calder, (2008), 'Assessing the Automaticity of Moral Processing: Efficient Coding of Moral Information during Narrative Comprehension', *Quarterly Journal of Experimental Psychology*, 62(1), pp. 41–9.
3. This quotation appears on numerous websites, but it was not possible to locate its origin.
4. Israel Zangwill (2010), 'Children of the Ghetto' (Milton Keynes: Lightning Source UK Ltd), book 2, chapter 16.

Appendix 1

Quick Test: Are You Narcissistic?

Give each of the ten statements below a number from 1 to 5 as follows:
1 strongly disagree **2** disagree **3** neutral **4** agree **5** strongly agree

1   I am very concerned with what others think of me.
2   I am easily bored.
3   I feel that I am attractive to the opposite sex.
4   I call or text my friends when we haven't spoken for a while.
5   People are always coming to me with their problems.
6   I am more important than most people I know.
7   I find that other people's remarks can be hurtful.
8   I don't like being alone for long.
9   People often don't appreciate me.
10 I feel that I am always sorting out people's problems for them.

Now add up all of your scores.
Scores between 24 and 34 are normal (the average is 29).
If your score is 35 or more you may be narcissistic.
If your score is 23 or less you may be lacking in self-confidence.
Please note: The above tests may give a preliminary indication of narcissistic tendencies or certain other personality traits that might be associated with a personality disorder, but professional help should be sought for a full evaluation.

Appendix 2

Quick Test: Are You Codependent?

Give each of the ten statements below a number from 1 to 5 as follows:
1 strongly disagree 2 disagree 3 neutral 4 agree 5 strongly agree

1 It seems to me that I am controlled by others.
2 I feel responsible for the behaviour of others.
3 I find it difficult to see situations or individuals realistically.
4 When I receive praise from others I feel more secure.
5 I often feel angry or hurt.
6 I often feel lonely.
7 It is difficult for me to say no when people ask me to do something.
8 I give up my interests in order to take part in activities that my friends enjoy.
9 I have an overwhelming urge for others to like me.
10 I need to feel needed.

Now add up all of your scores.
Scores between 21 and 37 are normal.
If your score is 38 or more you may be codependent.
If your score is 20 or less you may be narcissistic.
Please note: The above test may give an indication of codependency. It is not considered to be a personality disorder. If you are concerned you should seek professional help for a full evaluation.

Index

Titles of publications are in *italics*.

transferring problems from home
24–5
see also teamwork

Zimbardo, Philip 12